The Other Fellow May Be Right

The Civility of Howard Baker

Bill Haltom

Copyright ©2023 by William H. Haltom Jr.

All rights reserved. No part of this book may be reproduced or utilized in any form or by any means, electronic or mechanical, including photocopy, recording, or by an information storage and retrieval system, without permission in writing from the publisher.

Library of Congress Control Number: 2023918740

ISBN: 979-8-9873201-8-1

Printed and bound in the United States of America by Ingram Lightning Source

Third Edition
Edited by: Jacque Hillman, Kim Stewart
Layout and design by: Kim Stewart

The HillHelen Group LLC
470 North Pkwy. Suite C
Jackson, TN 38305

The HillHelen Group LLC
635 North 65th Place
Mesa, AZ 85205

(731) 394-2894
www.hillhelengrouppublishers.com
hillhelengroup@gmail.com

In memory of
Claude Galbreath Swafford
(1925–2016)

Author's Note

This book was completed in early 2014, when Senator Howard H. Baker Jr. was alive and well. I am honored that he reviewed the final manuscript and gave it his blessing. Senator Baker passed away on June 26, 2014.

CONTENTS

Prologue: An Uncivil, Divided Nation		1
1	A Civil Moment	7
2	A Father's Advice	15
3	The Education of a Civil Man	21
4	Civil Litigation	27
5	A Bipartisan Coalition Begins	33
6	The Beginning of the Two-Party System	43
7	The Luxury of an Unexpressed Thought	49
8	An Eloquent Listener	55
9	One-Man, One-Vote, Two Senators	59
10	Game, Set … Bipartisan Match	65
11	A Bipartisan Environment	69
12	Asking the Right Questions	77
13	An Eloquent Observer	89
14	Saving the Panama Canal	93
15	The Unmaking of the President, 1980	103
16	A New Office Does Not Require a New Office	109
17	A Rose for Mrs. Packwood	119
18	The Baker's Dozen	123
19	Saving the President	131
20	A Gentle Tennessee Wit	147
21	The View from Both Ends of Pennsylvania Avenue	151
22	The Cherry Blossom Romance	157
23	To Form a More Perfect Union	161
24	Ambassador Baker: Civility on the World Stage	165
25	A Bipartisan Celebration	173
26	Is 'Bakeritis' Fatal?	177
Epilogue: Baker School Will Keep Senator's Legacy Alive		181
Acknowledgments		185
Sources		189
Notes		193
About the Author		207

We live in a political atmosphere now in which common civility seems about to join chivalry in extinction, an atmosphere in which we argue for the sake of argument and accuse for the sake of advantage, an environment in which the adversarial process has become not a means to an end but an end in itself.

In this atmosphere, the adversarial system leads not to accomplishment but to entropy, not to policy but to paralysis.

I believe we have to start thinking about things a little differently in this country. While holding fast to our own principles, we must have a decent respect for differing points of view.

We must understand that after the time of testing comes the time for uniting. We must recognize that it is the resolution of conflict—rather than the perpetuation of conflict—that makes the difference between successful self-governing and civil warfare.

—Senator Howard Baker

When you understand the other fellow's point of view, and he understands yours, then you can sit down and you can work out your differences.

—President Harry Truman

PROLOGUE

An Uncivil, Divided Nation

On January 6, 2021, a mob of over 2,000 supporters of President Donald Trump attacked the United States Capitol building in Washington, DC.[1] They looted and vandalized the Capitol. They assaulted Capitol Police and Metropolitan Police officers. One hundred thirty-eight officers were injured, and four of those died by suicide within the next seven months.[2]

The mob sought to prevent Congress from counting the Electoral College votes to formalize the election of Joseph Biden as president of the United States.[3]

For weeks after Biden won by over seven million popular votes and seventy-four electoral votes, President Trump refused to concede the election. He claimed it was "rigged" and had been stolen from him.[4] State and federal judges rejected such claims in over fifty lawsuits filed by President Trump and his allies challenging the election results.[5] Even President Trump's own Attorney General said that the president's claim of a rigged election was not true.

President Trump urged his supporters to come to the Capitol

on January 6 and "stop the steal."[6] At a rally that day, he told them to march to the Capitol and "peacefully and patriotically make (their) voices heard." But he also urged them to "fight like hell," adding "and if you don't, you aren't going to have a country anymore."[7]

The protest at the Capitol was not a peaceful and patriotic display. It was a riot.[8] Using the stems of American flags, they bashed windows and doors. They breached police perimeters and sought Speaker Nancy Pelosi and other congressional leaders, perhaps to capture or even harm them. One group erected a gallows on the west side of the Capitol and chanted "Hang Mike Pence," after Pence rejected President Trump's assertions that the vice president could overturn the election results.

The Capitol was evacuated. The vice president, congressional members, and staff took cover for hours. After order was restored, they approved the Electoral College results and Biden's election as the 46th president of the United States.[9]

The tragic events of January 6, 2021, were a culmination of years of incivility in American public life, and private life as well.[10] Bullying, road rage, and countless other examples of hostility and anger had become common occurrences in an uncivil nation. Civility was increasingly regarded as weakness, not strength. Rancor in the workplace, school playgrounds, sports, and entertainment had become the norm.

Political campaigns were increasingly vicious. In Congress and state legislatures, members on both sides of the aisle not only refused to work with one another, but attacked their opponents personally.

There had been some bipartisan efforts to reverse this trend. Most notable was The Civility Project, launched in 2009 by Mark DeMoss and Lanny Davis.

DeMoss was a Republican and evangelical Christian who had been an aide to Moral Majority founder Jerry Falwell. Davis was a Democrat who had been an adviser to President Bill Clinton. DeMoss and Davis were close friends. Alarmed by the ferocious tone in American politics, they created The Civility Project to promote respectful political discussion and debate.

They drafted a civility pledge that was simple and to the point: "I will be civil in my public discourse and behavior. I will be respectful of others whether or not I agree with them. I will stand against incivility when I see it."

DeMoss and Davis sent the pledge to every member of Congress and every sitting governor in the United States. Five hundred eighty-five letters went out, simply asking senators, representatives and governors to review the pledge, sign, and return it to The Civility Project's offices in Atlanta. The plan was to take out full-page ads in major newspapers across America listing the names of everyone who signed the pledge.

Only three recipients signed it. They were Senator Joseph Lieberman, independent, of Connecticut; Representative Frank Wolf, Republican, of Virginia; and Representative Sue Myrick, Republican, of North Carolina.

To their surprise, DeMoss and Davis received a number of hostile responses. There was not just an unwillingness to sign the pledge, but open opposition to it.

The Civility Project was over.[11]

While Americans claimed in public opinion polls to be alarmed by the decline in civility, the growing notion was that civility and collegiality were qualities of losers. Many Americans seemed to agree with the late Leo Durocher's famous observation that "nice guys finish last."

But not so long ago, civility and collegiality and teamwork were cherished American values.[12]

They were the values of what Tom Brokaw accurately described as "the Greatest Generation" that won the Second World War and then returned home to build an affluent society.

They were values found in the White House and in the halls of Congress, in governors' mansions and in state legislatures. They were values of an era when many leaders from opposing political parties were friends and tried, without compromising their principles, to work together in a bipartisan effort to promote the general welfare.

It was a time when our most effective leaders, both in the public and private sector, understood the importance of strategic civility, a leadership approach that encouraged collaboration.

One of the greatest exemplars of this civility was a United States senator from Tennessee. For over forty years, he was a leader in the most contentious arenas of American life: courtrooms, political campaigns, the halls of Congress, and the White House. In all these venues, he practiced the art of strategic civility that brought adversaries together, finding agreement often to their surprise. And in this process, the senator and his colleagues on both sides of the congressional aisle achieved extraordinary bipartisan accomplishments.

The senator was Howard H. Baker Jr. of Tennessee, and to this day, he remains a role model of what strategic civility can accomplish.

This is the story of his civil life.

Senator Howard Baker Jr. and Senator Robert Byrd. Reprinted with the permission of Senator Baker and the Baker Center.

CHAPTER 1

A Civil Moment

Early on the morning of January 5, 1977, fifty-one-year-old Senator Howard H. Baker Jr. arrived at his new office.[1]

Senate office S-231 is on the principal floor of the United States Capitol. Next to the White House, S-231 was then and is now the most historic suite of offices in Washington, DC.

S-231 is the oldest occupied space in the Capitol.

When the United States House of Representatives first convened in the new Capitol building on November 17, 1800, they met in the large, spacious room that would later be labeled S-231.

When the House moved into its new quarters in the South Wing of the Capitol in 1804, S-231 became the first Library of Congress, housing over 3,000 volumes.

When the British invaded Washington in 1814, they used the books as kindling when they set the Capitol ablaze.

In 1825, Vice President John C. Calhoun occupied S-231, although he sometimes had to share the office with President John Quincy Adams since no room in the Capitol had been set aside for the chief executive.[2]

From 1860 to 1935, S-231 was the "Robing Room" for the United States Supreme Court. Over the years it was frequented by some of the nation's most famous jurists including Oliver Wendell Holmes, Louis Brandeis, and William Howard Taft.

In 1959, Senator Everett Dirksen of Illinois was elected Senate minority leader. Dirksen and his staff moved into S-231 as well as the adjoining offices in S-232. From 1959 until his death in 1969, he served as Senate Republican leader from this three-room suite.[3]

Everett Dirksen was Howard Baker's father-in-law. And on this cold January morning, as the 95th Congress convened, Baker moved into his father-in-law's old office as the newly elected minority leader of the United States Senate.

Baker had arrived in Washington ten years earlier, in 1967, after having made history in the Volunteer State. Baker was the first Republican from Tennessee elected to the United States Senate.

Baker was a congressional legacy.[4] (William Hillenbrand, the secretary of the Senate, jokingly referred to Senator Baker as "a congressional brat.") His father, Howard H. Baker Sr., served in the House of Representatives from 1951 until his death in 1964. His stepmother, Irene Baker, had completed his father's unexpired term in the House. And having married Joy Dirksen in 1951, Baker was not just a senator. He was a senator-in-law.

Being a legacy can be both a blessing and a burden.[5] Overlooking the historic accomplishment of a Republican being elected to the United States Senate from the traditional Democratic stronghold of Tennessee, some senators privately dismissed Baker as a "junior grade Everett Dirksen."

But early in his Senate career, the young Tennessean had shown remarkable independence and a tendency toward bipartisanship.

In May 1967, the new junior senator from Tennessee had aligned with Senator Edward Kennedy of Massachusetts in opposing his father-in-law's efforts to dilute the impact of the United States Supreme Court's "one man-one vote" decision in *Baker v. Carr*.[6]

That historic decision had emanated from Tennessee, where the rural-dominated legislature had not reapportioned election districts for over sixty years, denying blacks, urban residents, and Republicans representation in proportion to their percentage of the population. Senator Dirksen was concerned that *Baker v. Carr* might undermine the powerbase of mid-western Republicans. But when he attempted to in effect reverse *Baker v. Carr* by legislation, the minority leader of the United States Senate found himself opposed by his son-in-law. Respectfully opposed, but opposed.

Baker's colleagues in the Senate immediately noticed not only his bipartisanship. They also admired his friendly and easygoing style. Steve Roberts, who covered Capitol Hill for the *New York Times*, observed, "Senator Baker reflected certain values—bipartisanship, respect for the institution, a sense of civility, and a belief in the value of compromise."[7]

Baker was a true conservative who fervently believed in limiting the power of the federal government.[8] He was a "hawk" on foreign policy in general and the Vietnam War in particular. He admired and supported President Richard Nixon and had given the seconding speech for his nomination at the 1972 Republican National Convention. But as *The Almanac of American Politics* observed, Baker was "not a man who (could) be pinned down easily to an ideological label." He consistently supported civil rights legislation, often observing that he was an East Tennessee Republican who was proud to be a member of the party of Lincoln.

(East Tennessee had stayed with the Union during the Civil War. When the Tennessee Legislature had voted in 1861 to join the Confederacy, Senator Baker's home county, Scott County, had voted to secede from Tennessee!)

> "Senator Baker reflected certain values—bipartisanship, respect for the institution, a sense of civility, and a belief in the value of compromise."
>
> —*New York Times*

Baker had teamed with Senator Edmund Muskie, a liberal Democrat from Maine, in co-sponsoring the two most significant environmental laws ever enacted, the Clean Air Act and the Clean Water Act of 1970.⁹

In 1971, Senator Baker had turned down a his-for-the-asking position on the United States Supreme Court, responding to a White House inquiry conveyed by Attorney General John Mitchell. Baker said he was very happy serving in the Senate and preferred to stay there. The nomination had gone to William Rehnquist.¹⁰

In 1973, Baker had become a media star as the ranking Republican on the Senate Watergate Committee, asking his now famous compound question, "What did the president know, and when did he know it?"

He had given the keynote address at the 1976 Republican National Convention, and after the speech, had emerged as the favorite to be President Gerald Ford's running mate in the upcoming battle with Jimmy Carter. But to Baker's extreme disappointment, Ford had picked Senator Bob Dole instead. Even before the convention ended, Baker and his family made a quick departure back to Tennessee, the senator vowing to his close adviser, A.B. Culvahouse, "I will never again be a candidate in a one-vote election."¹¹

And now, six months later, Howard Baker was sitting in his father-in-law's old office, having won a 38-vote election the previous day to become minority leader of the United States Senate.¹²

Baker's election as Republican leader came on his third try for the office. He had first run in 1969, following the death of his father-in-law, but had lost that race to Senator Hugh Scott of Pennsylvania. It had been one of the few mistakes in his Senate career, as the young senator came across to his older colleagues as perhaps too much of a young man in a hurry.¹³

In 1971, he had challenged Senator Scott again for the

Republican leadership position, only to be rejected again by his GOP Senate colleagues.

And now, somewhat to his surprise, he had been elected as a reluctant candidate on his third attempt. He had defeated Senator Robert Griffin of Michigan thanks to a Bakeresque coalition of liberal Republicans such as Edward Brooke of Massachusetts and Richard Schweiker of Pennsylvania, moderates including Robert Packwood of Oregon, and conservatives, notably Pete Domenici of New Mexico. Baker also had the support of the "Class of 1977," all twelve newly elected freshman Republican senators.

As he sat in his new office, the new Senate minority leader faced a daunting task, a challenge greater than his father-in-law had ever faced in his years as leader. Baker had only 38 Republicans to lead in the United States Senate. Newly elected Democratic President Jimmy Carter had a veto-proof majority.[14]

Baker had a choice. He could go negative, leading the loyal Republican opposition in fighting the initiatives of the new administration. Such an approach might have laid the groundwork for Baker's own pursuit of the presidency in 1980. The other option was to lead the opposition on many issues, but to find bipartisan approaches that could get things done for the country without compromising bedrock Republican principles. True to the leadership style he had shown during his first ten years in the Senate, the new minority leader chose the second option.

But to pursue that option with any success, Baker had a tough assignment. He had to build a working relationship with a fellow senator who was also starting his first day in a new job. That senator was Robert Byrd of West Virginia. On the previous day, as Senator Baker was elected minority leader, Byrd was chosen by his Democratic colleagues as majority leader.[15]

Howard Baker and Robert Byrd could not have been more different in personality and political philosophy.

While Baker was a fiscal conservative, Byrd was dedicated to bringing federal projects to the State of West Virginia, earning him the title "King of Pork."

While Baker had supported the extension of the Voting Acts Right, the Fair Housing Act, and other civil rights legislation, Byrd had opposed them.

And perhaps most significantly, Baker and Byrd took dramatically different approaches to their work on the floor of the Senate and in committees. Baker was not a man to get bogged down in Senate rules, an approach he disliked as form over substance. Byrd, on the other hand, was the master of parliamentary procedure and technical Senate rules. He was known to ruthlessly use those rules to his tactical advantage, often to the surprise of his Senate colleagues.

> *"It was a plan of strategic civility: You don't surprise me, and I won't surprise you."*

Howard Baker knew that with only 38 votes, he had to figure out a way to work with the majority leader who had over 60 votes, a Democratic president, an encyclopedic knowledge of Senate rules, and a willingness to use them to his partisan advantage.

And so, on his first morning as minority leader, Baker developed a plan.[16] It was a plan of strategic civility. First, he would approach Byrd and offer him a deal. "You don't surprise me, and I won't surprise you," Baker suggested.

Byrd hesitated at first, saying, "I'll have to think about it." But after thinking, he said yes.

In the years to come, Byrd would sometimes violate his no-surprise promise, but not very often. And when he did, Baker would gently remind him of the agreement they had made on their first day together as co-leaders of the Senate.

Second, Baker knew something very important about Bob Byrd.[17] As much as Byrd loved the Senate and politics, there was something he loved even more. He loved to play the fiddle.

And Baker knew something else about Byrd's ambition. He knew that Bob Byrd had long dreamed of performing on a stage other than the Senate. Byrd wanted more than anything in life to play the fiddle on the stage of the Grand Ole Opry in Nashville.

And so the new minority leader of the United States Senate began to work on a plan to make Byrd's dream come true.

Baker would contact his friend and country music legend, Roy Acuff, and ask him to invite the majority leader of the United States Senate to play the fiddle on the stage of the Ryman Auditorium in Nashville. When that dream-come-true moment happened several months later, the minority leader of the United States Senate would be standing on the Opry stage, alongside his now good friend, Bob Byrd.[18]

But there was plenty of history to be made before that moment. On January 5, shortly after noon, the new minority leader of the United States Senate left office S-231 and walked to the floor of the United States Senate.[19] He entered through the famous bronze doors on the east side, and walked down the center aisle to the well of the Senate. There he met the newly elected majority leader, Robert Byrd, future star of the Grand Ole Opry. Baker and Byrd shook hands and exchanged pleasantries. They would repeat this gesture at the start of each meeting of the United States Senate over the next eight years.

It was a civil moment. But it was not a spontaneous or impulsive event. The genesis of that moment had occurred over 40 years earlier, when a very young Howard Baker received some advice from his father.

Senator Howard Baker and his sister Mary. Reprinted with the permission of Senator Baker and the Baker Center.

CHAPTER 2

A Father's Advice

Howard Henry Baker Jr. was born on November 16, 1925, the first child of Howard and Dora Ladd Baker. Senator Baker is fond of saying that he "cut his teeth on politics."[1] In fact, he cut it on law as well.

His grandfather, James Francis Baker, became a lawyer in 1886. He established a firm in Huntsville, a small town in the mountains of East Tennessee. By the 1890s, he had built a thriving law practice and was the publisher of a newspaper, *The Cumberland Chronicle*. He was a successful businessman. "He was the last Baker to make money," his grandson would recall. He was elected district attorney general and later became a judge.[2]

Howard Henry Baker Sr. was born on January 12, 1902. He would be Howard H. Baker Jr.'s role model for life.

Baker Sr. was an extraordinary lawyer and a natural born leader.[3] He first excelled as an undergraduate at the University of Tennessee. There he co-captained the debate team with Ray H. Jenkins, who later became a renowned trial lawyer. In 1954, Jenkins served as chief counsel to the Senate committee investigating

Joseph McCarthy's charges that Communists had infiltrated the United States Army.

Baker Sr. was elected president of the University of Tennessee Class of 1922. After graduating, he entered the university's law school, where he served as the first editor-in-chief of the *Tennessee Law Review*. After obtaining his law degree, he married Dora Ladd, the daughter of the sheriff of Roane County, Tennessee. He returned to Huntsville to practice law with his father.[4]

Baker Sr. became a successful lawyer and a leader who helped build two high schools, the Scott County Courthouse, the electric co-operative, and a bank.

Baker Sr.'s leadership style was congenial and affable. Senator Baker would fondly remember how his father interacted comfortably with all the people of Scott County, whether they were rich or poor.

When Baker Jr. was only eight years old, he faced the biggest challenge of his young life. His mother died suddenly after gallbladder surgery.[5]

In the aftermath, another unique role model would emerge for the boy. At his father's request, young Howard's maternal grandmother, Lillie Ladd, moved in with the family to help raise Howard and his sister Mary.

It is an understatement to say "Mother Ladd" (as Baker would call her) was a strong woman. She had been the first female sheriff in Tennessee, and had become something of a legend in East Tennessee after capturing five prisoners who had escaped from the Roane County jail.[6]

Mother Ladd, who lived to be 102, was alive and well in 1980, when Senator Baker told her that he was going to run for president. Her response was, "Well, if you really want power, you should come back to Tennessee and run for sheriff."

The Bakers were Republicans, a party allegiance that dated back to the Civil War.[7] On June 8, 1861, the good people of

Scott County had voted overwhelmingly against secession from the United States. When the Tennessee legislature ignored them and voted to secede from the Union, Scott County seceded from the State of Tennessee. The County Court approved a resolution forming the "Free and Independent State of Scott."

The resolution was not repealed until 1986, prompting Howard Baker Jr. to reflect that he was not really the senator from Tennessee, but rather the senator from the Free and Independent State of Scott.

In 1936, ten-year-old Baker Jr. accompanied his father on a tour of Tennessee to support Governor Alf Landon of Kansas for president.[8]

In 1938, the twelve-year-old made another trip with his father across the Volunteer State, as Baker Sr. ran for governor as the Republican nominee.

And in 1940, at age fifteen, Baker Jr. accompanied his father on yet another tour of the state, this time to support his father's candidacy for the United States Senate.

They were quixotic campaigns.

As a Republican in a staunchly Democratic state, Baker Sr. had no chance of winning a statewide election. It would not be until 1966 that another Republican named Howard Baker would make history by accomplishing that. Young Baker enjoyed touring the Volunteer State with his father, and snapped pictures along the way with his camera, pursuing a hobby he would enjoy for the rest of his life.

In 1951, Baker Sr. would be rewarded for his long and dedicated service to the Tennessee Republican Party by being elected to Congress in the second congressional district.

Young Howard Baker grew up watching his father in the courtroom and on the campaign trail.[9] He watched his father interact with folks in Huntsville and Scott County and across Tennessee. He observed how his father brought people together in a jury trial or a political campaign or a community effort to build a school, a bank, or a business.

Along the way, Baker Sr. gave his son some very good advice on how to get along with people and persuade and motivate them.[10]

"You should go through life always working under the assumption that the other fellow may be right," he told the boy. "He may be wrong, but you should listen to him and have a healthy respect for his point of view."

Howard H. Baker Jr. would remember and follow this advice for the rest of his life.

*"You should go through life
always working under the assumption
that the other fellow may be right.
He may be wrong,
but you should listen to him and
have a healthy respect for his point of view."*

—*Howard Baker Sr.*

Howard H. Baker Jr. at the McCallie School. Reprinted with the permission of Senator Baker and the Baker Center.

CHAPTER 3

The Education of a Civil Man

In the fall of 1941, Howard Baker Sr. drove his 15-year-old son to Chattanooga and enrolled him in the McCallie School, a military prep school. Baker Sr. felt that his inquisitive son needed a greater academic challenge than had been provided by his high school in Huntsville.[1]

Young Howard Baker would remember his first night at McCallie as perhaps the loneliest time of his life.[2] As he tried to fall asleep in his dorm, he kept thinking, "I am here by myself!"

Howard Baker would later remember his two years at McCallie as "the turning point in my life."

While he was not fond of the military drills and found the rigorous academics at McCallie challenging, he matured and began to enjoy his independence. He served as photography editor for both the student newspaper and the yearbook, continuing to develop the avocation of his life.[3]

In May of 1943, Baker graduated from McCallie. America was at war, and as Baker later recalled, "I had three choices. Get drafted, join the Army, or join the Navy. I picked number three."[4]

Baker joined the V-12 Program, a training project designed to supplement the Navy's force of commissioned officers.[5]

This was an incredible opportunity for Baker and his contemporaries. The Navy would provide an enlistee with two years of college education. He would then be sent to Midshipmen's School for a four-month course, after which he would be commissioned as an ensign in the US Navy Reserves.

Between 1943 and 1946, more than 125,000 men availed themselves of the V-12 Program, attending some 131 colleges and universities across the nation. The V-12 Program along with the post-war GI Bill made a college education a dream come true for the "Greatest Generation."

Future Ensign Baker would not have to travel far from home. The Navy sent him to the University of the South, at Sewanee, Tennessee.[6] Baker felt right at home on the mountaintop campus. Sewanee seemed much like his hometown of Huntsville, if Huntsville had a classic university like Oxford or Cambridge.

Baker studied electrical engineering in Sewanee, and it fascinated him.[7] It appeared he might forego the family tradition of law and politics.

"I planned to be an engineer and grow enormously wealthy with an invention," Baker recalled.

After a year at Sewanee, the Navy sent him to Tulane, where he studied electrical engineering, and enjoyed the nightlife in the "Big Easy." In 2005, he would return to New Orleans as *Ambassador* Howard Baker to give a speech at the city's World Trade Center. He told the audience, "I'd like to tell you all those things about my college days in this city. But the truth is the closest I got to international affairs back then was gaining a working knowledge of the French Quarter."[8]

After Tulane, Baker went to Midshipmen's School. Upon completion, he received his commission as lieutenant, junior grade.

In 1945, Baker was then sent to patrol torpedo boat school in

Rhode Island. Soon he was given a command of a PT boat, and he headed for the Pacific.

His war tour was a short one.⁹ Suddenly there was news from Hiroshima and then from Nagasaki. The Japanese surrendered, and Baker's PT boat turned around and headed to San Francisco. At the tender age of nineteen, Baker then spent a month in the City by the Bay "getting thrown out of every good bar I tried to get in."

While in San Francisco, Baker met another young ensign who had been commissioned through the V-12 Program.¹⁰ His name was Robert F. Kennedy, and their paths would cross again in Washington, DC, during the Army-McCarthy hearings and later when they would serve together in the United States Senate.

While Baker's Navy service was relatively brief, he regarded it as a critical part of his education.

In Midshipmen's School, PT boat training, and his brief tour in the Pacific, Baker learned more about the art of strategic civility that he would deploy in the coming years.

In 2002, some fifty-six years after his discharge from the Navy, Baker boarded the *USS Kitty Hawk* in his official capacity as ambassador to Japan. The *Kitty Hawk* was docked in Okinawa, and Ambassador Baker was invited to come aboard and address his fellow sailors. After being introduced by an admiral, the ambassador joked, "I still get nervous when I see all these gold braids." And then reflecting on his Navy days, he said, "I learned the value of teamwork. I learned that almost nothing of great significance happens without the confluence of the good faith efforts of men and women committed to the same objective."¹¹

It was another lesson that Baker would remember for the rest of his life.

In the fall of 1946, following his discharge from the Navy, Howard Baker arrived on "The Hill"—as Tennesseans refer to the campus of their state university.¹² Baker intended to continue his studies in electrical engineering at the University of Tennessee.

When he arrived at registration, he found long lines of veterans enrolling thanks to the GI Bill. Baker got in line to register for the College of Engineering and waited. And waited and waited and waited. At the end of the day, just as Baker was getting to the front of the line, the lights in the room began to flicker, and suddenly Baker realized that registration was closed.

A frustrated Baker left the building, got in his car, and started to drive back to Huntsville. He was not sure if he would ever return to "The Hill."

But as Baker drove away, he noticed the lights were on in the law school building. Baker parked his car and entered the law school. There was no line. He went to what appeared to be a registration desk and asked if he could register for law school. He was immediately admitted, conditioned only upon a subsequent review of his transcripts from Sewanee and Tulane.

Baker drove home to Huntsville and told his father that he had enrolled in law school.

"My father was stunned and thrilled!" Baker said.[13]

The family tradition of law was to continue.

Over the next three years, Baker pursued his law degree, although he did not particularly enjoy law school or give it his full attention. He joined Pi Kappa Phi fraternity and became immersed in extracurricular activities, particularly student government.[14]

In 1948, Howard Baker made his first run for political office.[15] He announced his candidacy for president of the student body. Baker's first campaign was a preview of those he would wage for the United States Senate some twenty years later. While he was a Greek, Baker campaigned on the theme of bringing independents and Greeks together. At the heart of this issue was a jukebox in the school gym. The jukebox was under the control of some strong-willed Greeks, to the exclusion of the independents. Candidate Baker promised that if elected, the independents would have the same access to the jukebox as did the fraternities and sororities.

Baker also promised to establish a campus radio station.

On April 26, 1948, Baker's "All Students" ticket swept to victory.[16] President Baker then spent his final year of law school delivering on his campaign promises.

In early 1949, WUOT, the campus radio station Baker had promised, made its first broadcast.[17]

Over sixty years later, WUOT was still on the air, broadcasting from the campus of the University of Tennessee as part of the National Public Radio network, sending its listeners classical music, *Prairie Home Companion*, and *Car Talk*.

Baker had no idea whatever happened to the jukebox.

After graduating from law school, Howard Baker joined his father's law firm. Reprinted with the permission of Senator Baker and the Baker Center.

CHAPTER 4

Civil Litigation

In the summer of 1925, just a few months before Howard Baker's birth, hundreds of Tennesseans as well as newspaper reporters from around the country descended upon the Rhea County Courthouse in Dayton, Tennessee.[1]

They packed the galleries to watch the trial of John Thomas Scopes, a twenty-four-year-old football coach who agreed to be indicted for violating a Tennessee law that banned the teaching of evolution. Never mind that Coach Scopes was simply a substitute teacher who couldn't recall ever teaching evolution. Like football, it was just a game to Coach Scopes, who had been recruited by the American Civil Liberties Union and several "progressive" leaders in Dayton to set up a heavyweight legal battle between legendary trial lawyer Clarence Darrow and world-famous orator William Jennings Bryan.

Thirty years after this "trial of the century," folks in East Tennessee were still packing the courtroom galleries to watch jury trials. And the lawyer they came to watch was young Howard Baker.[2]

After graduating from law school in 1949, Howard Baker

returned to Huntsville and joined the firm of Baker and Baker, the law firm his grandfather had started in 1886. His father insisted that the newest Baker lawyer start practice in general sessions court, in effect the Class A baseball of trial courts, where the smallest claims were litigated.

The young lawyer also took on a load of criminal cases. Years later he would recall, "My very best clients were in jail. Sometimes I was hired by someone who was yelling out the jail window as I was walking to lunch."[3]

After trying a few cases solo in the general sessions and criminal courts, Howard Baker Jr. joined Howard Baker Sr. as they tried a jury case together. Baker Sr. deferred to Baker Jr. to do the closing argument. Then Howard Henry, as his father called him, delivered a closing summation that was more classical oratory than East Tennessee common sense.

When the trial was over, his father gave him a critique: "You were all right," he said, "but the clarity of your words sometimes exceeds the wisdom of your thoughts."[4]

Young Baker took note. He began to address juries with a conversational style that he would use later on the campaign trail and on the floor of the United States Senate.

Soon the word began to spread through Tennessee courthouses. Baker was emerging as "the outstanding young lawyer in East Tennessee," in the words of the great trial lawyer Ray H. Jenkins.[5]

Baker loved being in the courtroom. Decades later, even after his service as a senator, White House chief of staff, and ambassador, Baker said he enjoyed law more than any part of his career.[6]

Thanks in large measure to his grandfather and father, he inherited some very rich and powerful clients, including the Southern Railroad, utility interests, coal and lumber companies.[7]

But the clients he loved the most were generally those who could not afford to pay him a penny. They were clients who desperately needed him because they had been charged with murder.

Howard Baker loved defending capital cases. He tried sixty-three such cases over seventeen years.[8] Years later he reflected on the impact of that time.

"Till this day there is nothing I can think of that has a more riveting effect on your attention and is a greater challenge to your ability than to try to defend somebody in a capital case. It really is an extraordinary responsibility," he said.[9]

Not everyone in Huntsville appreciated the young lawyer's willingness to take on such extraordinary responsibilities. When Baker agreed to defend a local scoundrel named Bob Lambert, Baker got a visit from his best friend, Bill Swain. Swain was also Baker's best client as he was head of Swain Lumber Mill. Swain pointed out to Baker that Bob Lambert was guilty as sin. He had shot a man in front of several witnesses, and after doing so had asked, "Is he dead?" Rather than waiting for an answer, he had shot the victim again.

When Swain advised Baker he should dismiss such an awful client, Baker responded, "Bill, in our legal system everyone is entitled to representation."[10]

Lambert was not acquitted, but he wasn't sent to the electric chair as the prosecutor sought. Not one of Baker's sixty-three capital case clients was ever given the death penalty.

There were two keys to Baker's effectiveness as a trial lawyer.[11] First, he got along well with opposing counsel, even the prosecutors in the capital cases.

"We were fellow circuit riders," Baker observed. He and his adversaries would battle each other in the court all day and then enjoy drinks and dinner together at night.

The other key to his success as a trial lawyer was his courtroom style.[12] He was particularly effective at the art of cross-examination, using a style that appeared so friendly even to adverse witnesses that they ended up saying a lot more from the witness stand than they should have.

Jurors loved Howard Baker.

"Juries just trusted him," said his law partner, Don Stansberry. "He was just so credible."[13]

In 1954, Baker briefly left the courthouses of Tennessee to go to Washington to serve as an assistant to Ray H. Jenkins, chief counsel for the Senate committee investigating Senator Joseph McCarthy's charges that Communists had infiltrated the United States Army.[14] The assignment also renewed his friendship with Robert F. Kennedy, the fellow V-12 ensign he had met in San Francisco in 1945. Kennedy was the committee's minority counsel. Baker was excited about the assignment until, as he later recalled, "I realized that my only duty was to read daily transcripts." He quickly returned to his life as a busy Tennessee trial lawyer.

Baker's effectiveness as a lawyer was based in large measure on what he believed the law is really all about. Baker felt that while cases and trials are by definition contentious, the real purpose of the law is to resolve conflicts, not to create them. In a 2005 television interview, Baker summarized his belief in the rule of law:

> The rule of law is an interesting phrase. I don't think it's ever really been defined with exactitude. But to me, the law is the lattice work that civilization uses for ordering people's relationships with each other and to govern their conduct. That is the law. The law is not statute law, the law is not precedent, it's not Supreme Court decisions, or any other court's decision. The law is an accumulation of the determination of mankind to find ways to get along, to respect each other, to have a decent respect for different points of view, and to translate disagreement into some sort of resolution. That's what the law is. And without the law, we would not have civilization.[15]

Baker loved being a lawyer, and the very civil nature of his approach before judges and juries made him incredibly effective. While Baker Sr. was in Washington serving in Congress, young Howard Henry was more than happy to be running the Baker family law practice, and he saw this as his life's work.

On January 7, 1964, Baker was in Washington arguing a case before the Federal Power Commission. The proceedings were interrupted when Baker's father-in-law walked into the hearing room. Senator Dirksen took Baker aside and broke the news that Howard Baker Sr. had suffered a fatal heart attack.[16]

With his father's passing, Howard Baker was about to enter a new era of his life. After fifteen years in the courtroom, he was about to enter a new and even more contentious arena, politics.

His stepmother, Irene, headed to Congress to fill out Howard Baker Sr.'s unexpired term. Howard H. Baker Jr. then made a bold move. On May 26, 1964, he announced that he was a candidate for the United States Senate.

Senator Baker on the campaign trail, 1964. Reprinted with the permission of Senator Baker and the Baker Center.

CHAPTER 5

A Bipartisan Coalition Begins

By the spring of 1964, thirty-six-year-old John Seigenthaler had already become the most influential journalist in Tennessee.

In 1949, he had been hired as a reporter for the *Tennessean*, Nashville's morning paper, joining a staff that included future Pulitzer Prize winners David Halberstam and Tom Wicker.[1]

Seigenthaler's flamboyant reporting style not only won him national journalism awards. It made him a Tennessee celebrity and the subject of national news coverage, as reporters in effect covered the reporter.

Most notably, in 1954, he covered the developing story of a man who was threatening to commit suicide by jumping off a Nashville bridge. Seigenthaler saved the man's life, grabbing him by the collar as he attempted to plunge.[2]

Seigenthaler's reporting on corruption in the Teamsters led to the prosecution and ultimate conviction of Jimmy Hoffa.

In 1957, Seigenthaler went to Washington at the request of the young lawyer whom Howard Baker had first met as a fellow

Navy ensign in San Francisco in 1945 and had worked with in the Army-McCarthy hearings.[3]

Robert Kennedy, unlike Baker, had not left Washington after the McCarthy hearings. He was now chief counsel of the Senate Committee on Labor-Management Improprieties, better known as the "McClellan Committee."

The future attorney general was aggressively investigating corruption in labor unions. He had learned about Seigenthaler's investigative reporting on Hoffa and the Teamsters.

Seigenthaler gave Kennedy a bound volume of his *Tennessean* articles, recounting the lawless behavior of the Teamsters in Tennessee. It was an understatement to say that Kennedy was impressed. He pronounced Seigenthaler's work "dynamite," and requested his assistance on behalf of the McClellan Committee.

It was the beginning of a friendship and an association between Kennedy and Seigenthaler that would last through Kennedy's 1968 presidential campaign until his tragic assassination in Los Angeles on June 6, 1968.

When Kennedy became attorney general in January 1961, Seignethaler accompanied him to the Justice Department to serve as his administrative assistant.

During his service as the top assistant to the attorney general, the journalist once again made national news. In the summer of 1961, Kennedy dispatched Seigenthaler to Montgomery, Alabama, to negotiate police protection for the Freedom Riders. This group of young black college students were courageously making a bus trip through the South to desegregate public transportation. In the process, Seigenthaler himself had been brutally attacked by an angry mob.

The horrible scene was caught on film and was broadcast on the nightly network news, making Seigenthaler a folk hero in the Civil Rights movement.

In 1962, Seigenthaler returned to his hometown of Nashville.

The *Tennessean*'s new publisher, Amon Carter Evans, named Seigenthaler as the paper's new editor.

Seigenthaler was a liberal Democrat, and in its fifty-seven-year history, the *Tennessean* had never endorsed a Republican for statewide office.

But on a spring morning in 1964, Howard Baker walked into the offices of the *Tennessean* and introduced himself to John Seigenthaler. Seigenthaler was surprised and impressed by Baker's opening line.[4]

"I know the *Tennessean* will never endorse me, and I understand that," Baker said, after shaking Seigenthaler's hand. "I just wanted to come by, introduce myself, and ask you what you think I should be doing in my campaign."

Seigenthaler smiled, and had to suppress a laugh. *He's a very nice young man*, Seigenthaler thought. *Too bad he doesn't have a chance.*

Seigenthaler's skepticism about Baker's candidacy was based on the reality of Tennessee politics.

In 1964, Tennessee remained a staunchly Democratic state. The Volunteer State had not elected a Republican governor in nearly fifty years, and it had never elected a Republican senator. Tennessee was such a Democratic state that in over one-third of its 95 counties, Republicans did not even hold primaries. They simply did not contest local elected offices.

Tennessee Republicans traditionally held power only in Baker's East Tennessee, "the Grand Division" of the state that sided with the Union in the Civil War and never left the Party of Lincoln.

West and Middle Tennessee had long been ruled by Democrats, and for decades, statewide elections had essentially been controlled by one Democrat, Edward H. Crump of Memphis, who was known as "Boss Crump."[5]

From 1932 to 1948, Boss Crump's hand-picked slate of candidates had won every Tennessee statewide election.

Crump had died in 1954, and over the next ten years, a

bipartisan coalition had begun to evolve in Memphis. The headquarters of this coalition had been in the law offices of a man named Lewis Donelson. In the early 1950s, Donelson was probably the unlikeliest man in Tennessee to develop a statewide Republican Party.[6] He was the great-grandson of Andrew Jackson Donelson, nephew of President Andrew Jackson, creator of the national Democratic party.

Lewis Donelson grew up in Memphis during the Depression, a time when the only Republicans in the state's largest city were a small group of African Americans led by Lt. George Washington Lee, famously known as "Lt. Lee of Beale Street."

After graduating number one in his class at Georgetown University Law School, young Donelson returned home to Memphis and began to establish a dynamic and influential law practice.[7] His law firm would grow to be the largest and most powerful in the state.

The young attorney initially eschewed politics, focusing on his law practice. But he had strong opinions about his hometown of Memphis, a city that had no two-party system. The city was run by Boss Crump. There was no evidence that Crump was corrupt, and the city's trains, or more accurately, its trolleys, ran on time. But in Lewis Donelson's eyes, his hometown was a benevolent dictatorship.

One evening in late 1951, Donelson attended a cocktail party where he and his fellow guests became engaged in a discussion about one of his favorite topics, politics. Donelson sounded off on how the Democratic Party had left the South. He decried how it was "almost impossible for a southerner to be considered for the presidency, and the Democrats gave the South a token vice presidential spot to salve wounds and preserve the one-party southern vote."[8]

On a roll, Lewis Donelson noted the impact of the one-party system on his hometown and his native state. All Memphis and statewide elections were decided in the Democratic Primaries, "often contested not over issues, but personalities." The lack of competition, Donelson believed, "produced a lower quality candidate and officeholder than we deserve."

Donelson believed that "the continuance of the one-party system would doom the South to perpetual inferiority in the national picture."

One of the guests at the party that evening was Allen Redd, a Memphis businessman.[9] A few days after the party, Redd called Donelson and invited him to lunch. Hoping to gain Redd as a client, Donelson agreed. But when Donelson and Redd met, Redd wanted to talk politics, not business.

"You ought to be a Republican," Redd told a surprised Donelson. "I am trying to organize some Memphians to revive the Republican Party in Shelby County to create a true two-party system."

"It never occurred to me up until now that I might not be a Democrat."

—*Lewis Donelson*

Donelson responded, "That's a big move for me. I'm almost like Andrew Jackson's great-great grandson, and it never occurred to me up until now that I might not be a Democrat."

But Donelson promised to think it over, and went home and discussed it with his wife, Jan.

Donelson and his wife agreed that it was the right thing to do, even if it had a negative impact on his growing law practice.

Donelson called Allen Redd and agreed to join him in an effort to create a modern Republican Party in Memphis and in Tennessee. Donelson then began to call his fellow lawyers, friends, and clients to advance the bold idea that they should join him in becoming Republicans. While the suggestion alarmed some, it intrigued others.

It particularly intrigued some of his fellow young lawyers including Harry Wellford and John Thomason.[10]

It also got the favorable attention of young businessmen like Dan Kuykendall and a dentist, Dr. Winfield Dunn.

Donelson and his colleagues formed a group called "the New Guard Republicans."[11] The New Guard emerging in Memphis would not initially win the support of the Old Guard Republicans in East Tennessee.

"They really didn't like us," Donelson said. "They were content to control two congressional districts in East Tennessee, leaving the other seven congressional seats, both Senate positions, the governor's mansion, and the legislature in the control of Democrats."

But the New Guard Republicans in Memphis began to get some unlikely allies.[12] Memphis Mayor Edmund Orgill, attorney Lucius Burch, and *Memphis Press Scimitar* Editor Edward Meeman were all liberal Democrats. They had taken on Boss Crump as early as 1948, in support of the candidacy of Estes Kefauver for the United States Senate. Kefauver had been elected by winning the Democratic Primary over Boss Crump's candidate. It was the first political defeat Boss Crump had ever suffered.

Four years later, in 1952, Boss Crump would suffer his second defeat when liberal Albert Gore defeated eighty-three-year-old Senator Kenneth McKellar, the powerful chairman of the Senate Appropriations Committee, who was seeking his seventh term.

By the late 1950s, the New Guard Republicans were filling slates of candidates for the state legislature and local offices. While they weren't winning, they were getting a surprising number of votes.

In 1962, New Guard Republican candidate Bob James came within just a few thousand votes of defeating twelve term-Democratic Congressman Clifford Davis. Republican hopes statewide were further emboldened that year with the election of Bill Brock, a Republican from Chattanooga, to Congress in the third congressional district.

By early 1964, Lewis Donelson and the New Guard Republicans had put together a bipartisan coalition of new Republicans from Memphis, longtime Republicans from East Tennessee, conservative Democrats who didn't like Lyndon Johnson and were inspired by Barry Goldwater, and African Americans such as Lt. Lee of Beale Street who remained true to the Party of Lincoln.[13]

This bipartisan coalition was ready to make history. All it needed was a candidate.

In Sevierville, Tennessee, attorney John Waters was confident he had found that candidate.[14] In fact, he had already seen him campaign and win what could be called a statewide election.

In 1948, Waters had been a freshman at the University of Tennessee. There he had met a law student named Howard Baker, candidate for student body president. Waters had worked in this first Baker campaign, helping him forge the coalition between Greeks and independents. It was the beginning of a lifelong friendship.

On a winter day in 1964, Waters met his friend at a restaurant in the Farragat Hotel in downtown Knoxville.[15] Baker was still grieving over the death of his father. Friends had urged him to run for his father's congressional seat, but he declined, telling his stepmother, Irene, she should run. Baker had managed his stepmother's campaign in a special election to fill his father's term, just as he had managed each and every one of his father's campaigns for Congress since 1950. Irene Baker had been elected, and it appeared that Howard Henry was ready to return to law practice as the new senior partner of Baker and Baker.

But Waters had another idea. He urged his old friend to run for the open United States Senate seat that had become available due to the death of Senator Estes Kefauver the previous summer.

In Memphis, Lewis Donelson was reaching the same conclusion.[16] He was confident that Baker was a candidate who would appeal to the bipartisan coalition of the New Guard, the Old Guard in East Tennessee, and disaffected Democrats across the state who were ready for new leadership.

Donelson drove to Knoxville, where he joined Waters and

George Edd Morton of the State Republican Executive Committee and renewed Waters's call that Baker run for the Senate. Baker was initially skeptical.

"We are going to have a huge turnout in Shelby County (Memphis)," Donelson assured him. "And that coupled with votes in East Tennessee is going to surprise some people!"

Baker asked for a little time to consider the matter. A few days later, he called his old friend, Waters.

"Johnny, if you manage my campaign, I'll run," Baker said.

The campaign was on.

Baker later reflected that he really had "no particular expectation of winning."[17] In a sense, he was being the good Republican soldier his father had been when he ran for the United States Senate in 1938 and had received less than 30 percent of the vote.

Baker's opponent in the race was Congressman Ross Bass, a liberal Democrat who had served five terms as representative from Tennessee's Sixth District and had a solid base of support in Middle Tennessee. Bass, like most Southern Democrats, had signed the infamous Southern Manifesto of 1956, a commitment to segregation in opposition to the Supreme Court decision in Brown v. Board of Education. The Congressman had later apologized for the vote and became a supporter of civil rights, voting for the Civil Rights Act of 1964.

Howard Baker's campaign style was unique in Tennessee political history. He eschewed the traditional approach "of coming around to a town and swapping stories with the old courthouse regulars." He was more likely to be found in television stations in Memphis and Nashville and Knoxville and Chattanooga rather than in rural courthouses.[18]

Baker understood the new medium of television and realized that it wasn't about classic Southern oratory, but about sound bites. Moreover, television was free campaign advertising. While a speech in the courthouse square might reach 100 people, an appearance on the local TV news could reach 100,000.

Baker was a natural for the emerging new political age. His campaign speeches were presented in the casual and informal style he had perfected in courtrooms to persuade judges and juries.

For a man who was self-effacing, he seemed to be an incredible retail politician. John Waters marveled at how Baker could work the room at small gatherings.[19]

"He wasn't a glad-hander or boisterous," Waters recalled. "He was a listener. He impressed people by giving them his undivided attention."

"He was just so credible," Donelson noted. "He was trustworthy and believable."[20]

> *"He was a listener. He impressed people by giving them his undivided attention."*
>
> *—John Waters*

There were no daily tracking polls in 1964, but by mid-October, political observers across the state were sensing that there could be an upset. True to its Democratic tradition, the Tennessean had endorsed Congressman Ross Bass, but John Seigenthaler was impressed with Baker's campaign style and had a gut feeling that Baker represented the future of Tennessee politics.[21]

Baker himself had entered the campaign with no real thought that he would win. But years later, he would recall that a few weeks before Election Day, "it dawned on me that you might just mess around and win this thing."[22]

And then, the Republican nominee for president, Senator Barry Goldwater, came to Tennessee.[23]

When Goldwater's plane landed in Knoxville, Baker escorted him to a campaign platform and gave him a rousing introduction to thousands of East Tennessee voters.

But to Baker's surprise and chagrin, Goldwater told the crowd that if he was elected president, he would "sell TVA."

TVA, the Tennessee Valley Authority, was a sacred cow in

Tennessee politics. It may have been the employer of half the crowd assembled at the Knoxville airport.

Baker later recalled that when he heard Goldwater's promise to sell TVA, "I could see my prospects going right down the drain. I sat there on the platform wishing that, instead of introducing Goldwater, I had said, 'Senator Goldwater has asked me to say a few words on his behalf.'"

On Election Day, the expected Bass victory occurred. But the margin was narrower than anyone had predicted. Ross Bass had won 568,905 (52.1%) to Howard Baker's 517,330 (47.4%). [24]

Baker had won more votes than any GOP candidate in Tennessee history.

The bipartisan coalition had fallen short, but John Seigenthaler's hunch was right. A new era had begun in Tennessee political history, with Howard Baker as its leader.

CHAPTER 6

The Beginning of the Two-Party System

Frank G. Clement was the foremost Tennessee politician of his generation. By 1966, many Tennesseans were surprised that he was still in the governor's mansion. By that time, they expected that he would be in the White House.[1]

Frank Clement had taken the Volunteer State by storm in 1952. The political boy wonder had been elected governor at the age of thirty-two.

Clement was a spellbinding orator with the style of an evangelical preacher. Indeed, his campaign rallies had the feel of revivals, and he would close his speeches with the words of the Thomas Dorsey spiritual:

> Precious Lord, take my hand
> Lead me on, let me stand
> I am tired, I am weak, I am worn
> Through the storm, through the night

Lead me on to the light
Take my hand, precious Lord, lead me home.[2]

In 1956, he had been selected to give the keynote address for the Democratic National Convention in Chicago. He brought the delegates to their feet with his rhetorical question, "How long, O Lord, how long?"[3]

Many regarded him as the William Jennings Bryan of his generation, and his speech almost propelled him to a vice presidential nomination. (It would ultimately go to his fellow Tennessean, Senator Estes Kefauver.)

Many Tennesseans truly believed that it was just a matter of time before Frank Clement would join Andrew Jackson and Andrew Johnson on the list of Tennesseans who had resided in the White House. Clement had been easily re-elected governor in 1954 and in 1962.

Clement's long ambition was to go to Washington, if not as president, then as a senator. He had been upset by Ross Bass in the Democratic primary in 1964, but in 1966 he had defeated Bass and was ready to fulfill his destiny. The only person standing between him and the United States Senate was Howard Baker. Despite the surprise showing against Bass in 1964, Baker was regarded as the decided underdog.

But Governor Clement had two problems.[4]

First, the very flamboyant campaign style that had propelled him to power in the early 1950s was going out of style. As *The Almanac of American Politics* observed, Clement's "hand-waving, lecturn-thumping, florid oratorical style . . . used to liven up a hot afternoon on the courthouse square, but in the age of television campaigning, it was obsolete."

The other problem was more significant. The worst-kept secret in Tennessee politics was that Clement had a drinking problem.

Knoxville Journal Publisher Guy Smith had a picture of Clement

Senator Baker on the campaign trail, 1966. Reprinted with the permission of Senator Baker and the Baker Center.

in which the governor clearly appeared quite inebriated. Under Smith's instructions, every story the *Knoxville Journal* ran about the governor would be accompanied by that unflattering picture.[5]

Baker was appalled by the picture and told his staff in no uncertain terms that they should never use it, or make any references to the governor's personal issues in the campaign.

The truth of the matter was that Baker liked and admired the governor.[6] Baker and Clement had first met in 1949 when Baker was a new lawyer and Clement was counsel to the Tennessee Railroad and Public Utilities Commission. Clement had freely given young Baker advice on how to handle matters before the powerful commission. Baker had always been grateful for this.

And so in the fall of 1966, Clement was still holding his revival meetings in the courthouse square.

Baker was running a very civil campaign.

Before his fall campaign against Governor Clement, Baker faced a challenge he had not faced in 1964—a contested Republican Primary.[7] Ken Roberts, a tall, handsome young banker from Nashville, had served as Tennessee campaign manager for Goldwater for President in 1964. Roberts jumped into the campaign in early 1966 portraying himself as the true conservative against the moderate Baker. Roberts's not-so-subtle campaign theme was that Baker, like his father, had been a good soldier as a Republican nominee for the Senate in 1964, but it was Ken Roberts who was positioned to make history by actually being elected in 1966.

Baker refused to debate Roberts or respond to the charges that he was a moderate.[8] He simply continued the style of his 1964 campaign, focusing on the media with television interviews and meetings with newspaper editors. It paid off, as he won primary endorsements from the *Chattanooga Times*, the *Memphis Press-Scimitar* and, of course, the *Knoxville Journal*. Baker also drove across the state in a rented Greyhound bus, stopping and talking with voters at homes, diners, businesses, and factories.

Roberts's campaign appeared to be better financed and organized than Baker's.[9] But on primary Election Day in August of 1966, two things happened. First, an unprecedented number of Tennesseans voted in the Republican Primary. And second, they voted overwhelmingly for Baker.

To the surprise of even some of the New Guard Republicans, Baker easily beat Roberts with seventy-seven percent of the vote. Harry Wellford, who served as Baker's West Tennessee campaign manager in 1966 just as he had done in 1964, regarded the Roberts challenge as a blessing.[10] The hard-fought contest energized the emerging Republican Party in Tennessee, giving nearly two hundred thousand Tennessee voters the opportunity to identify themselves as Republicans. Moreover, Roberts's portrayal of Baker as a "moderate" helped Baker in developing the bipartisan support he needed to defeat Governor Clement.

Baker sought to expand the bipartisan coalition by seeking the support of African Americans in Memphis and Nashville.[11] In his 1964 campaign, Baker had said he would have voted against the Civil Rights Act of 1964 as an unwanted intrusion of power by the federal government. But by 1966, Baker freely admitted to Dr. Benjamin Hooks and other African-American leaders that he regretted that position. For the rest of his public life, Baker would be an ardent supporter of civil rights.

He sought to make inroads in the labor community. Having long secured the vote in his native East Tennessee, he focused on Middle and West Tennessee, particularly Memphis where his friend Dan Kuykendall was on the verge of making history by winning the ninth district congressional seat.

And through it all, Baker ran a civil campaign, adamantly refusing to go negative against the governor whom he actually found to be a sympathetic figure. And in response, Governor Clement could not figure how to go on the offensive.[12]

"How do I attack Howard Baker," he asked, "who's never been elected anything except president of the student body at the University of Tennessee?"

The governor's son, Bob Clement, who would later be elected to Congress, would remember the 1966 Senate campaign as one of the cleanest elections he ever saw.

And then in October, just weeks before the election, the *Tennessean* made an unprecedented move. It endorsed Howard Baker for the United States Senate.[13]

Two years earlier, in their first meeting, Baker had assured John Seigenthaler that he knew the *Tennessean* would never endorse him. It may have been just a characteristically self-effacing remark. But it may have been strategic civility, and if so, it had worked.

On Election Day, Baker made history.

He beat Clement by nearly 100,000 votes.

Thirty-six years later, Lewis Donelson summarized this historic event: "People say that the two-party system in Tennessee began the day Howard Baker was elected to the Senate. But actually, the two-party system began a few weeks before the election, when John Seigenthaler and the *Tennessean* endorsed him."[14]

CHAPTER 7

The Luxury of an Unexpressed Thought

In early 1964, Howard Baker was in Washington on legal business. Late in the day, he had some extra time before he was to catch an early evening flight to Knoxville, so he dropped by the office of his father-in-law, the minority leader of the United States Senate, Everett Dirksen.[1]

Baker and the senator were discussing the minority leader's favorite topic, his grandchildren. Their conversation was interrupted when the senator's secretary came in and told him, "The president is on the phone."

Baker started to leave, but his father-in-law motioned for him to stay seated.

Baker then heard one end of the conversation: "Hello, Mr. President." Pause. "I am sorry, Mr. President, but I can't come down to the White House after work for a drink." Another pause. "Well, I'll tell you why I can't come. I did that last night, and we got to talking. I came home late—and Luella was mad."[2]

Luella was the grandmother of Howard Baker's children.

Baker thought to himself at the time, "What a remarkable exchange. Here is the Republican leader of the Senate and a Democratic president of the United States who have been friends and colleagues for years, speaking in such a personal way."[3]

A short time later, Howard Baker started to leave and head for the airport.

At that moment, he heard a clatter in the reception area of the minority leader's office.

Baker would later vividly recall what happened:

> The door flung open, and I saw two Beagle dogs tied onto one leather leash. At the other end of the leash was the president of the United States.
>
> The first thing he said was, "Well, if you won't come drink with me, I'll come drink with you." The president and senator retired to a private room in the back of the Republican leader's office. At that point, I was not invited to attend and did not.[4]

Baker was impressed.

As he entered the United States Senate in January 1967, he would vividly remember the image of his father-in-law and President Lyndon Johnson visiting together and retiring for drinks. And long after his own service as minority leader, Senator Howard Baker would observe:

> To this day I don't know what issues they dealt with or what problems they solved. Given their long relationship of mutual respect, I'm sure they saw some—and perhaps many.
>
> But I've always thought of that as an example of how the system should work—high controversy,

Senator Baker and his father-in-law, Senator Everett Dirksen. Reprinted with the permission of Senator Baker and the Baker Center.

fierce competition of ideas, energetic debate, but in the final analysis, preserving personal relationships and a decent respect for different points of view.[5]

During his first two years in the United States Senate, Baker had his father-in-law as a mentor. Dirksen became the role model for Howard Baker the senator just as Howard Baker Sr. had been the role model for Howard Baker the lawyer.

Dirksen was one of the most flamboyant and colorful politicians Washington had ever seen. There were some issues on which he would absolutely not compromise. The most notable of these was his commitment to make the marigold the national flower.[6]

In one of his last speeches on the Senate floor, in March of 1969, the minority leader of the United States Senate spoke in support of his favorite cause:

> Most important of all, I must not forget the marigold. For ten years I have sought to persuade the Congress to adopt the marigold as our national floral emblem. Some prefer the rose or the carnation or the petunia, violet, daffodil, or some other bloom. But the marigold is native to this hemisphere and grows in every one of the 50 states, evidence of a robustness against the elements or insects that is unequaled in performance by any other flower.[7]

He was also fond of saying, "You just can't beat a marigold for humility." It was that type of speech that endeared him to his Senate colleagues.

But the marigold-as-national-flower was one of the few causes in which Dirksen was uncompromising.

Dirksen was a very practical legislator who was always looking for a bipartisan solution. He once explained, "I'm a man of principle, and one of my principles is flexibility."[8]

Dirksen approached issues cautiously. He did not wish to draw lines in the sand. He would listen to his colleagues and take notes. He asked questions showing a genuine interest in what his fellow senators had to say, regardless of which side of the Senate aisle they sat on.

When he would begin to formulate his own positions on issues, he would do so with caution and a willingness to reconsider. After Dirksen's death, his son-in-law would write of him, "Virtually every idea he held, he held tentatively. The world would be better off if more people did that these days."[9]

Senator Everett Dirksen's leadership style as minority leader can be summarized in one word: civility.

He was civil to the president of the United States, whether that president was a Republican Dwight Eisenhower, a Democrat John F. Kennedy, or a Democrat Lyndon Johnson.

He was civil with his Senate colleagues, even in the midst of fierce debates.

As Baker would recall, Dirksen always had a decent respect for the opposing point of view.

He respected the institution of the Senate, and he felt it was more important than the minority leader or any individual senator.

And he absolutely enjoyed being a member of what he truly believed was the world's greatest deliberative body.

He was also the proprietor and chief bartender of the Twilight Lodge, the bar in the minority leader's office where he entertained his fellow senators with drinks at the close of the legislative day. It was the Twilight Lodge to which the senator and the president of the United States had retreated on that 1964 day as future Senator Baker headed for the airport.[10]

> *"Senator, occasionally allow yourself the luxury of an unexpressed thought."*
>
> —Everett Dirksen

From 1967 until Senator Dirksen's death in 1969, the young senator from Tennessee took notes. He watched the man who was the grandfather of his children, father of his bride, and arguably the most powerful Republican United States senator of his generation.

The impressionable young senator watched and learned.

In the spring of 1967, Senator Howard Baker gave his maiden speech on the floor of the United States Senate. The topic was revenue sharing.

At the end of the speech, the young senator was surrounded by his colleagues. They shook his hand, patted him on his back and congratulated him on a very fine talk.

The minority leader of the United States Senate sat a few feet away, saying nothing.

Finally, Baker approached his father-in-law.

"Well, Senator, what did you think of my speech?" Baker asked.

Dirksen paused briefly. Then he looked the new freshman senator in the eye and said, "Senator, occasionally allow yourself the luxury of an unexpressed thought."[11]

The young senator got the message. Leaders should speak less and listen more.

It was a lesson he would remember for the rest of his years in the United States Senate.

CHAPTER 8

An Eloquent Listener

John Waters was convinced that it was Senator Howard Baker's greatest gift as a leader.

"He is an incredible listener," Waters said. "He's the world's greatest listener, in fact!"[1]

Waters recalled that in the first Baker Senate campaign in 1964, the young candidate would seldom glad-hand a crowd. He would not work a room of voters by telling them what he was going to do for them if he got elected. He would introduce himself, ask questions, and listen.[2]

After his election in 1966, he continued to use the same style on his visits back to Tennessee.

"He would call me and tell me there was an issue coming before the Senate, and he needed to discuss it with the folks back home," Waters said. "He would ask me to set up a meeting in my office with several of us who had worked in his campaign."[3]

When Senate Baker arrived at the meeting, he would briefly tell the assembled group the issue he wanted addressed. And then, rather than telling them his position on the issue, he would ask the attendees what they thought. He would listen to them attentively and make notes. Sometimes at the end of the meeting, he would summarize what people had said.

His friend Bill Swain laughed about this.

"When Howard summarized what we said, it always sounded better than how we had said it!" Swain said.

And then, Senator Baker would thank the folks for their comments.

"He would often leave the meeting without telling us what his position was," Waters said. "But when it came time for him to vote on the issue, we all felt we had been heard, even if he took a position different from ours."[4]

Senator Baker took the same approach in Washington. His colleagues in the Senate noted his unique style.

"There was a quietness there that was part of his demeanor in absorbing what was going on," recalled a fellow senator.[5]

He tried to avoid direct confrontation with his Senate colleagues, even when he disagreed with them.[6] A Senate staffer would remember Baker on one occasion responding to an adversary by calmly saying, "It seems to me that we may have to do just that, but I wonder if it might not be better if first we . . ."

And then, in a non-confrontational manner, he would summarize comments made by other senators, quietly building his own case for the action that should be taken.

The senator also developed a unique approach to lobbyists. When a hotly contested issue was coming before the Senate, Baker would direct his assistant, Ron McMahon, to contact the best lobbyist on each side of the issue. The senator would then meet with both lobbyists separately. He would listen, ask them questions, and gather information.[7]

He did not see lobbyists as a source of campaign contributions. He saw them as a source of information.

For Baker, listening was not just a part of leadership. It was the

Senator Baker meeting with constituents. Reprinted with the permission of Senator Baker and the Baker Center.

key to leadership. The senator would later summarize his approach:

> I increasingly believe that the essence of leadership, the essence of good Senate service, is the ability to be an eloquent listener, to hear and understand what your colleagues have to say, what your party has to say, what the country has to say. And the ability follows to try to translate that into useful policy.[8]

Senator Howard Baker was an eloquent listener.

The GOP freshman class of the United States Senate, 1967. Reprinted with the permission of Senator Baker and the Baker Center.

*"Howard, my only advice to you is this:
If you are going to fight, try to win."*

—Senator Everett Dirksen,
advising his son-in-law, Howard Baker Jr.

CHAPTER 9

One-Man, One-Vote, Two Senators

In 1962, the United States Supreme Court issued its landmark decision in *Baker v. Carr*.[1] That decision soon became known to both journalists and constitutional scholars alike as the "One-man, One-vote" decision.

In time, that decision would be regarded as "the most important and sophisticated political reform in American history."[2]

In *Baker v. Carr* and a series of related decisions, the nation's highest court had addressed the issue of the apportionment of representatives for state and congressional legislative bodies.

During the twentieth century, there was across the country a movement of the population from farms and small towns to cities. The shift in population meant that the cities could emerge as influential powers in the state legislatures and ultimately in Congress after reappointment following each decennial census.[3]

But throughout the nation, rural political power groups resisted this power shift by refusing to reapportion their legislative districts.

The states had a constitutional duty to reapportion according to their population. But the rural-dominated legislatures of many states ignored the constitutional duties. One of those states was Howard Baker's Tennessee.[4]

The Tennessee Constitution required the reappointment of both houses of the legislature on the basis of population. But the legislature had ignored this, doing no reappointments whatsoever since 1901.

Baker v. Carr originated in Memphis where a number of voters filed the lawsuit against the Tennessee Secretary of State claiming that the refusal to reapportion the legislative districts on the basis of population caused them to suffer a "debasement of their vote" and the denial of equal protection of the law as guaranteed to them by the Fourteenth Amendment of the United States Constitution.[5]

The district court dismissed the case, ruling in effect that voters had no legal right to challenge legislative apportionments.

But on March 26, 1962, in a 6-2 decision, the United States Supreme Court ruled that voters indeed had the right to challenge apportionment statutes as a violation of equal protection under the United States Constitution. The decision opened the floodgates to lawsuits by voters across the country challenging whether legislative and congressional districts fairly represented the voters.

One year after *Baker v. Carr*, the United States Supreme Court issued its decision in *Gray v. Sanders*, ruling that Georgia's system of giving more weight to rural voters in statewide district elections violated the Equal Protection Clause of the Fourteenth Amendment. The Court stated unequivocally that "all who participate in the election are to have an equal vote." The Court held that "the conception of political equality from the Declaration of Independence to Lincoln's Gettysburg Address, to the Fifteenth, Seventeenth, and Nineteenth Amendments can mean only one thing—one person, one vote."[6]

The following year, in *Wesberry v. Sanders*, the Supreme Court held that the principle of one-man, one-vote applied to congressional elections. The Court ruled, "The command of Article I Section 2, that representatives should be chosen by the people of the several states, means that, as nearly as practicable, one man's vote in a congressional election is to be worth as much as another's."[7]

And a few months after the *Wesberry* decision, the nation's highest Court ruled in *Reynolds v. Sims*, that the one-man, one-vote principle was applicable to state legislatures, as well as Congress.[8]

The series of one-man, one-vote decisions that began with *Baker v. Carr* sent shockwaves through the American political system. Congressional representatives of rural districts and their counterparts in state legislatures felt that the United States Supreme Court had in the words of one southern politician, "stopped preaching and gone to meddling."

When Howard Baker arrived in Washington in January 1967 as a freshman senator, a concerted effort was underway in Congress to stop the United States Supreme Court's intervention in congressional and legislative redistricting.[9] And leading this fight was none other than Senator Baker's own father-in-law, the minority leader of the United States Senate, Everett Dirksen.

Between 1964 and 1965, Senator Dirksen had introduced three bills in an effort to prevent Supreme Court intervention in congressional and legislative apportionment. He even called for a constitutional convention to consider enacting an amendment that would, in effect, reverse *Baker v. Carr* and its related decisions.

The Senate minority leader claimed that the one-man, one-vote decisions amounted to unwanted judicial intrusion into legislative issues. He told the *Wall Street Journal*, "The question is not one-man, one-vote, but whether the SOO-PREME Court can require it. If a legislature wants to do it, fine." (Dierksen took delight in always pronouncing the nation's highest Court the "SOO-PREME" Court.)[10]

As a freshman senator, Howard Baker was not expected to challenge or disagree with the Senate minority leader, particularly given the fact that that minority leader just happened to be his father-in-law.[11] But Senator Howard Baker supported the *Baker v. Carr* decision. He had witnessed how the rural-dominated Tennessee legislature had limited the voting rights and consequently the political power of citizens in the state's emerging cities, particularly Memphis. The growing city on the banks of the Mississippi was the center of the emerging new Republican Party of Tennessee. It was also the hometown of most of the state's African American population, and Howard Baker had seen how the Tennessee legislature was denying African Americans and Republicans representation in proportion to their numbers in the population.

The new senator's position on this issue was not a secret. In his campaign for the Senate in 1966, he had voiced unequivocal support for *Baker v. Carr*, saying that one-man, one-vote was the "principle tenet of Tennessee Republicanism." Nevertheless, when Baker arrived in Washington in the winter of 1967, few political observers felt he would take on his father-in-law on such a sensitive issue.

But Baker was about to show his independence, his bipartisanship, and also his civility. In early 1967, the freshman senator and the Senate minority leader met and "agreed to disagree without animus." They agreed they would not embarrass each other, and they would give each other prior notice if they sought to oppose the other on an issue. They also agreed to never ask the other for a vote on any issue.[12]

True to his word, in May of 1967, Senator Baker met with his father-in-law in the minority leader's office in the Capitol. He told him that he was firmly committed to the principle of one-man, one-vote, and he would oppose Dirksen's efforts to limit or reverse the Supreme Court decisions. The minority leader's response was to look his son-in-law in the eye and say, "Howard, my only advice to you is this: If you are going to fight, try to win."

Baker then joined forces with an unlikely ally, Senator Edward Kennedy of Massachusetts.[13] The rural-dominated House of Representatives had already passed a bill allowing a 30 percent deviation in population between the largest and smallest district in the state until 1970, and a ten percent deviation after 1970.

The battle then went to the United States Senate with veteran Senators Dirksen and Sam Ervin for the bill and young Senators Baker and Kennedy leading the opposition. Between them, Senators Dirksen and Ervin had nearly fifty years of congressional experience. Senators Baker and Kennedy had six.

The Washington press labeled the Dirksen-Baker battle a "political family feud."[14] But it was conducted in an entirely civil tone consistent with the two senators agreeing to "disagree without animus."

A bipartisan effort then emerged by Senators Kennedy and Baker. While Kennedy lined up the votes of Democrat senators, Baker lined up the Republicans.[15] It was not an easy task persuading Republican senators to oppose the minority leader on the apportionment bill. But just as he did during his eighteen years as a Tennessee trial lawyer, Senator Baker made an effective and persuasive case. He privately shared with the Republican senators the evidence that decades of malapportionment had helped Democrats, not Republicans. He shared statistics clearly indicating that if congressional seats were apportioned pursuant to one man, one-vote principles, the GOP would have won a lot more house seats over the years.

In the end, the young senators prevailed. They defeated the Dirksen-Ervin bill that would have diluted and circumvented the Supreme Court's one-man, one-vote decisions.

The press had a field day.[16] The *Washington Daily News* featured the headline, "Senate's Young Pup Lames Old Growler." The accompanying article stated that Senator Howard Baker had "handed his famous father-in-law, Senate minority leader Everett Dirksen, an astonishing licking on the Senate floor."

But the story of one-man, one-vote, and two senators in the spring of 1967 was not the story of a partisan legislative victory. It was the emerging story of a new young leader in the Senate who would reach across the aisle and work quietly and effectively in a bipartisan, collaborative effort to get things done. And in the process, that young senator was invariably civil, remembering both his agreement with his father-in-law and the advice of his father. He would disagree without animus and always respect an opposing point of view.

CHAPTER 10

Game, Set... Bipartisan Match

On April 17, 1967, freshman Senator Howard H. Baker Jr. of Tennessee took to the well of the Senate and threw down the gauntlet. He challenged his Democratic Senate colleagues to a duel... not with guns, but with tennis rackets.

The young senator's challenge had been inspired by an article in the April issue of the magazine, *Washingtonian*, which had listed the top five tennis players in Congress.[1] According to the *Washingtonian*, the Senate's best racket men were:

1. Senator Claiborne Pell
2. Senator Robert F. Kennedy
3. Senator Jacob K. Javits
4. Senator Birch Bayh
5. Senator Edward M. Kennedy

In mock seriousness, Senator Baker acknowledged at the beginning of his remarks that as a freshman senator, he was "not to be heard, and not (even) to be seen very much."[2]

The senator said that while he believed and observed the rule and had "great respect for the traditions of the Senate, tradition or no tradition, there comes a time when man can remain silent no longer." Baker pointed out that four of the five senators listed by the *Washingtonian* as the top tennis players were Democrats.

With tongue firmly in cheek, Baker announced that he and his fellow Republican freshman senators—Mark Hatfield, Charles Percy, and Edward Brooke—had met to determine what to do about the *Washingtonian* tennis listing that they regarded as unfair and highly partisan:

> We were concerned about what response would be most appropriate, and I must admit there was some initial disagreement in our group. There was a view that we should resolve the conflict by negotiating an honorable peace, and there was a view that we should accept the challenge not on the tennis courts, but escalate in a more forceful and militant manner.
>
> We asked for advice. Our senior colleagues were somewhat divided. The staff members in the Republican Policy Committee raised some rather serious questions about whether we should commit ourselves to a conflict which might be open ended.
>
> We nevertheless were able to agree to respond to the challenge with limited and measured force on the tennis courts.[3]

The new junior senator from Tennessee then challenged Democrats to a series of doubles tennis matches to resolve the issue of who were the greatest tennis players in the United States Senate.

On cue, Senator Joseph Clark, Democrat of Pennsylvania, asked Senator Baker to yield. Baker did so, and Senator Clark

Senator Howard Baker, Senator Walter Mondale, and Senator Edward Brooke. Reprinted with the permission of the Minnesota Historical Society.

then said that on behalf of "a united Democratic party on this issue . . . we accept the challenge." Senator Clark continued:

> I will be prepared to meet with the senator from Tennessee, in order to draw up appropriate rules for what I think might turn out to be the greatest Davis Cup match which ever took place, at least within earshot of the Capitol. Thus, I commit myself as the acting leader of the Democrats in the Senate in this regard, to meet with the senator from Tennessee and work out an appropriate procedure. I can assure him that I am not a bit surprised that there was a good deal of disagreement among our friends on the Republican side of the aisle; but, on this issue, there will be absolutely no disagreement

among the Majority Party, which presently has somewhat tenuous control over procedures in this honorable body.

On September 28, 1967, The Great Senatorial Tennis Match took place as a fundraiser for the Washington Area Tennis Patrons Foundation which benefited poor Washington area youth who otherwise could not afford to play tennis.[4]

Senator Baker served as captain of the Republican team, with Senator Clark leading the Democrats.

Baker led his fellow Republicans onto the court wearing a beautiful tennis sweater with red and blue bands at the neck, bottom, and sleeves. Joy Baker had made it for the occasion.

Nationally syndicated humor columnist Art Buchwald of the *Washington Post* served as umpire. While his calls were not particularly accurate, they were funny.[5]

The event consisted of three doubles matches. Howard Baker and his partner, Senator Edward W. Brooke of Massachusetts, won their match in a six-to-four victory over Democrats Walter Mondale of Minnesota and Joseph Tydings of Maryland.

But it proved to be the only Republican victory of the day. Republicans Strom Thurmond and Charles Percy fell to Democrats Pell and Clark, and Jacob Javits and Pete Dominici were bested by Democrats Ernest Hollings and William Spong.

After claiming the first "US Senate Tennis Championship," Senator Clark offered the Republicans another chance next year.[6]

"We accept," said Senator Baker.

"It is a gracious and falsely confident offer," added Charles Percy, the Republican junior senator from Illinois.

Despite all the pre-match partisan bravado, it proved to be a wonderfully bipartisan day, typical of an era when Republican and Democratic senators were political adversaries, but nevertheless, close friends.

CHAPTER 11

A Bipartisan Environment

Howard Baker always loved Washington, DC. He had loved it since he first visited the Capitol in July of 1939, at the age of thirteen, on a family vacation en route to the New York World's Fair. His great-aunt, Mattie Keen, was secretary to Tennessee Senator Kenneth McKellar. She secured her nephew a gallery pass for the Senate, giving him his first glimpse of the arena where he would later lead.[1]

Baker loved Washington during his eighteen years in the Senate and his later years as White House chief of staff. Baker loved the history, the architecture, and the excitement of our nation's capital. But Washington, DC, was never his home. It was never the place he most loved and revered.

Home to Howard Baker was always Big South Fork Country.

The Big South Fork of the Cumberland River straddles the Kentucky-Tennessee border and the Cumberland Mountains of Northeast Tennessee.

Its mammoth gorges earned the area the nickname the "Yosemite of the East."[2]

It is a stunningly beautiful part of the world inhabited by hundreds of species of plants and animals.

In 1867, John Muir hiked the Cumberlands through Big South Fork Country, and he was inspired to found the Sierra Club, the nation's foremost conservation group.[3]

The Bakers have lived in Big South Fork Country for over two hundred years, and Howard Baker spent his life hiking through its mountains and canoeing its streams.[4]

A lot of folks who get elected to Congress move to Washington and never really come home except to campaign for re-election. And when their time in Congress ends, they often remain in Washington.

But not Howard Baker. During his years in public service, he got back to Big South Fork Country as often as he could. His longtime pilot and dear friend, Lonnie Strunk, could fly him from Washington back home in just a little over forty-five minutes.

In 1993, Baker published *Big South Fork Country*, a collection of his photographs of the home he loved.

In 1969, Baker's love for the mountains and streams of Big South Fork Country inspired him to lead a bipartisan legislative battle that culminated in the passage of the two most significant environmental laws ever enacted, the Clean Air Act of 1970, and the Water Pollution Act Amendments, otherwise known as the Clean Water Act.[5]

As he had done in the one-man, one-vote battle, Baker joined forces with an unlikely ally, Senator Edmund Muskie of Maine.[6]

Muskie was a Yankee liberal. Baker was a Southern conservative. While Muskie no doubt viewed clean air and water as a liberal cause, Baker saw it as a decidedly conservative one. He was a conservationist who wanted to preserve Big South Fork Country and other wilderness areas across the nation.

He explained this in the introduction to his photography book, *Big South Fork Country*:

Photo of Big South Country by Senator Baker. Reprinted with the permission of Senator Baker and the Baker Center.

> Here is conservatism at its most profound, but it's a personal rather than an ideological conservatism, the kind that springs from a genuine celebration of the world as it is, the kind that keeps people close to the earth and rejoices in life's simple pleasures.
>
> It's a conservatism less fired by political passion than warmed by a coal stove, but it's a rugged, protective philosophy all the same.[7]

Baker truly saw environmental protection as a conservative cause, designed not only to protect the air we breathe and the water we drink, but also to preserve a way of life. He was fond of quoting his cousin, James Toomey Baker, who proposed that their hometown of Huntsville, Tennessee, choose as its centennial theme "A Century of Status Quo."[8]

To further support environmental protection as a conservative issue, Baker would point out that the words "conservative" and "conservation" have the same Latin root.[9]

In 1969, conservative Senator Baker and liberal Senator Muskie began to work together to develop national standards for America's air and water and a scientific and technology-based means for meeting those standards.

The effort met immediate and strong resistance from interest groups and constituencies, particularly lobbyists for the auto industry. But the bipartisan coalition of Baker and Muskie worked to accommodate competing views.

Baker later praised Muskie's civility in the process:

> In every aspect of his legislative career, which I witnessed personally on the environment and the budget process and later in foreign policy, Ed Muskie was willing to work as long as it took with whomever was necessary—irrespective of

> party or point of view—to achieve a constructive public policy result. He believed that we could compromise without giving away principles. He knew that compromise—he called it comity—was the essence of a workable legislative process. And he knew that each of us had our ideas and our ideals, our interests, and our constituencies that, like his own, had to be accommodated.[10]

The result was one of the most concise pieces of legislation in Senate history.[11] The Clean Air Act of 1970 was only thirty-eight pages long. As Baker would later recall, it had five major provisions:

> First and foremost, we declared a direct and overarching federal interest in protecting the health of all Americans from air pollution.
>
> Second, we incorporated in law the concept of technology forcing.
>
> Third, we established deadlines for government action.
>
> Fourth, we made many of those government actions mandatory rather than permissive.
>
> Fifth, we empowered the public, individual American citizens, with the authority to use the federal courts to achieve the objectives we set forth should the bureaucracy or the politicians fail to do so.[12]

In the process, Baker showed his unique talent for using lobbyists as allies rather than adversaries. He and Muskie listened to, addressed, and in many cases accommodated competing points of view. And when the thirty-eight-page bill finally came before the United States Senate, it passed unanimously.

The Clean Air Act of 1970, and its sister, the Clean Water Act, are the legislative accomplishments Senator Howard Baker proudly regards as his "lasting legacy."

That legacy is preserved in the Big South Fork National River and Recreation Area, a federal reserve that Congress established in 1974 to protect Baker's beloved homeland.

In the introduction to *Big South Fork Country*, Baker wrote:

> Because the Big South Fork is a new federal reserve, only 800,000 visitors came to see us in 1992, compared with 8 million who journeyed to the Great Smokies two hours south of here. We think we can accommodate a few more than 800,000, but frankly, we don't want 8 million people a year tramping around in our mountains.
>
> We're going to share the secrets of the Cumberlands with you, but we would prefer you didn't mention it to anyone else.[13]

Thirty-five years after the passage of the Clean Air Act, a retrospective event was held at the Howard Baker Center for Public Policy at the University of Tennessee.

In his speech on that occasion, Howard Baker reflected on the lasting impact of the Clean Air Act and Clean Water Act:

> Like many of you here, I have visited many parts of the world which have not enjoyed the full benefits of the environmental revolution the initiation of which I am proud to have been a part.
>
> It is difficult to breathe the air in Beijing and other cities in China and many of the cities in Asia and in Eastern Europe, where pollution control has not been a primary national policy.

> We have seen our economy multiply; our automobile population multiply; our population multiply; the number of vehicle miles we travel multiply. And yet in every instance our air is still getting cleaner. We haven't achieved Ed Muskie's public health standards yet. But we have in place both a body of law and a national philosophy which should make that possible in our lifetime.
>
> We triggered a global change. As a result of our investment and the collective effort of a few committed men who gathered in a small committee meeting room, we charted a change in the course of history.[14]

Baker then concluded by noting that he had "always been struck by the fact that Thomas Jefferson insisted that his tombstone reflect only that he founded the University of Virginia—not that he was ambassador to France, or secretary of state, or vice president or even president of the United States. Not that he had drafted the Declaration of Independence, but that he had founded an institution of higher learning."[15]

Baker then added, "I'll be proud to have 'He wrote The Clean Air Act' on my tombstone."[16]

Senator Baker and Senator Sam Ervin. Reprinted with the permission of the United States Senate Historical Office.

"At that point, a light went on in my head, and I thought, 'Baker, maybe you don't know as much about this as you think you do. You better put your head down and follow the facts wherever they lead you.'"

—Howard Baker Jr.

CHAPTER 12

Asking the Right Questions

In March of 1973, Senator Howard Baker asked for a private meeting with the president of the United States.[1]

Baker had long admired and supported Richard Nixon. He had first worked in support of the president in the 1960 election, campaigning for Nixon not only in Tennessee with his father, but also in Illinois, with his father-in-law.

At the 1968 GOP Convention, at President Nixon's request, Senator Baker had given the nominating speech for Governor Spiro Agnew as Nixon's running mate.[2]

At the 1972 GOP Convention in Miami, Senator Baker had given the seconding speech for the president's nomination for re-election.

In November of 1972, Richard Nixon had won the greatest landslide in American presidential election history, carrying forty-nine of the fifty states.

But in the midst of the president's successful re-election campaign, a strange event had occurred. In the early morning hours of June 17, 1972, a security guard had found five men who had broken into the headquarters of the Democratic National Committee at the Watergate Hotel.

The episode had been initially dismissed by White House Press Secretary Ron Ziegler as "a third-rate burglary attempt." But the burglars had cash on them, and as the FBI agents followed the money, the trail led to the Committee to Re-Elect the President, and perhaps to the White House as well.

Little attention was paid to the story until after Election Day, 1972. But as the year grew to a close and a new year began, evidence began to mount that even if the president had no direct connection with the Watergate break-in, the White House may have attempted a cover-up of this and related scandals in the campaign.

In February 1973, the Senate had voted to establish the Senate Select Committee on Presidential Campaign Activities. Senator Sam Ervin of North Carolina was appointed the chair, with Senator Howard Baker as the vice chair.

Still an ardent supporter of Nixon, Senator Baker was not just skeptical about the charges that he and his fellow committee members were being asked to investigate. He honestly believed that the Watergate break-in may have been "a Democratic dirty trick—something staged to embarrass the president."[3] And so as the committee began to assemble a staff to conduct its investigation, Baker requested this meeting with a man who was not just his president, but an old friend.

The president and the senator met not in the Oval Office, but in the president's private office in the Old Executive Office Building.

They chatted for a few minutes. Then Baker reverted to his days as a lawyer. He decided to give his friend, the president of the United States, some advice.

"I told the president that as the senior Republican on the committee, I was going to see that his rights were protected during the inquiry," the senator would remember. "I said that there was enough lawyer left in me to advise him to put an end to the allegations and send his witnesses 'pounding on the door and demanding to testify.'"[4]

When the president did not respond to this suggestion, Baker continued, "As I reviewed what I knew about the situation, I ended by saying 'I hope my friend John Mitchell doesn't have a problem.' I had known John before he became attorney general, and had done some work with him when he was a lawyer in New York."[5]

Baker would never forget what happened next.

The president hesitated for a moment.

"Well, he may," Nixon said.[6]

This was a turning point in Baker's support of Nixon and his approach to the coming Watergate hearings.[7]

"At that point," Baker said, "a light went on in my head, and I thought, 'Baker, maybe you don't know as much about this as you think you do. You better put your head down and follow the facts wherever they lead you.'"

Baker left the Old Executive Office meeting that day determined to find the truth, however unpleasant the truth might be.

Not long after this meeting, Baker flew to Nashville to attend a luncheon sponsored by the Tennessee Accountants Association, where he was honored as "The Man of the Year."[8]

There was one non-accountant in the audience that day. He was a young lawyer named Fred Thompson. A former assistant US attorney, Thompson had served as Baker's Middle Tennessee campaign manager during his bid for a second term. On Election Day in November 1972, Richard Nixon was not the only candidate who had won by a landslide. Baker had been re-elected by a margin of nearly 300,000 votes.

After the senator's speech to the accountants, Thompson made his way to the dais to shake hands and wish him the best.

To Thompson's surprise, the senator asked if he would ride

with him to the airport. Thompson would later recount:

> It was a short ride to the airport, and the senator came right to the point.
> "Fred," he said, "I've been appointed vice chairman of the Watergate Committee."
> My mind raced for facts I felt I should have known. I remembered something in the papers about the resolution that had created the committee.
> Baker went on: "I'm considering several people for minority counsel of the committee, and you're one of them. I don't know what the pay is, but it won't be enough. It should last a few months, and the minority counsel will have a responsibility for supervising one-third of the staff. I want you to understand I'm not offering you the job, but I wanted to see what your reaction would be if we make that decision." [9]

Thompson was hesitant. He was trying to establish a new law practice in Nashville, and "a few months" in Washington could be a major career setback.

After consulting with his wife and a few close friends, Thompson sent a message to the senator: "If you want me for the job, I'll do it."

"Fred, you're it," Baker responded.

On the following morning, Thompson's wife drove him to the Nashville airport for his flight to Washington. Kissing his wife and kids goodbye, Thompson reassured them.

"I really don't think this thing will last more than a few months at most, and I should be able to come back and resume my law practice, at least part-time, by June or July," he told them. "Sometimes these so-called political scandals have a way of playing themselves out after a few days."

The young attorney had no idea he was about to be a witness to history.

On May 17, 1973, Senator Sam Ervin pounded his gavel in the Caucus Room of the Senate office building, calling to order the first session of the Senate Select Committee on Presidential Campaign Activities, now popularly known as "the Watergate Committee." As millions watched the nationally televised proceedings, Senator Ervin recognized the committee's vice chair. Baker made a brief opening statement, beginning with the observation that "there is no need to further emphasize the gravity of the matters that we begin to explore publicly here this morning. Suffice to say there are serious charges and allegations made against individuals, and against institutions. The very integrity of our political process itself has been called into question." The senator continued: [10]

> . . . We have a great burden to discharge and carry. This committee is not a court, nor is it a jury. We do not sit to pass judgment on the guilt or innocence of anyone. The greatest service that this committee can perform for the Senate, the Congress, and for the people of this nation is to achieve a full discovery of all the facts that bear on the subject of this inquiry. This committee was created by the Senate to do exactly that. To find as many of the facts, the circumstances, and the relationships as we can, to assemble those facts into a coherent and intelligible presentation, and to make recommendations to the Congress for any changes in statute law or the basic charter document of the United States that may seem indicated.
>
> And this committee can serve quite another important function that neither a grand jury investigation or a jury proceeding is equipped to

serve, and that is to develop the facts in full view of all the people of America. Although juries will eventually determine the guilt or innocence of persons who have been and may be indicted for a specific violation of the law, it is the American people who must be the final judge of Watergate. It is the American people who must decide, based on the evidence spread before them, what Watergate means, about how we should all conduct our public business in the future.

It was a classic opening statement, similar to the ones Baker had delivered in countless jury trials in Tennessee courtrooms. The jury was going to hear the facts as the witnesses testified and exhibits were produced.

Over the next several weeks, the American people did in fact see the facts develop. Baker emerged as a media star.

The senator's friend and future senator himself, Lamar Alexander, said at the time that the Watergate Committee hearings were "just Howard Baker doing the two things he does best—engaging in a head-on exchange and being on television."[11]

What the American people saw Senator Baker do during the hearings in the spring of 1973 was not just what jurors in Tennessee courtrooms had seen Baker do in trials in the 1950s and 1960s. It was what John Waters had witnessed Baker doing in small meetings on the campaign trail or with supporters, advisers, or even lobbyists as he was getting information on important issues.

Baker was asking questions. And he was asking the right questions.

But as Baker asked the right questions, he did exactly what his father-in-law Everett Dirksen had counseled him to do.[12] He listened. As he listened, he grew frustrated at both the equivocation of testimony and the lack of focus on the part of the committee.

He complained to his press assistant, Ron McMahon, that the committee had been "chasing rabbits, and we need to find the central animal." In a meeting with the minority counsel, the senator said, "Fred, you know this testimony is wandering all over the lot. But what we need to know, really, is the president's involvement. I think I'll ask a witness to elaborate on what he feels the president knew about this in advance."

And then, on the morning of June 28, 1973, Baker asked the most famous question of the Watergate hearing. The witness was John Dean, former White House counsel to the president. In what would become the most memorable moment of the hearings, the senator asked Dean: "What did the president know, and when did the president know it?" [13]

> *"In what would become the most memorable moment of the hearings, the senator asked: 'What did the president know, and when did the president know it?'"*

Fred Thompson described the moment:

"It was kind of like ringing a bell on a cold winter morning. There was clarity there, and it was a common sense question, because that's what everybody wanted to know." [14]

The right questions were being asked not only at the televised hearing. In their private investigation, Baker's staff members were also asking the pertinent questions. The forthcoming answers would ultimately lead to President Richard Nixon's resignation.

Before John Dean had testified, Fred Thompson had had a long conversation with Fred Buzhardt, the current White House counsel. Buzhardt had given Thompson in great detail the White House version of the president's conversation with John Dean and others. Thompson thought it sounded a little too detailed. How, he wondered, could Buzhardt provide such specific information about the president's supposedly private conversations with Dean and other aides? [15]

Don Sanders, the committee's deputy minority counsel, had a hunch.[16] Maybe, just maybe, the president's conversations with Dean and others had been recorded. Sanders's suspicion was based on something John Dean had said in his testimony. He recalled that at the end of one of his conversations with the president, he had been taken to a side of the Oval Office. The president had addressed him in a very low voice concerning a presidential exchange with Chuck Colson about executive clemency.

Why had the president taken Dean to another side of the Oval Office? And if it was just the two of them in the room, why did the president address him in a low voice?

The suspicion on Sanders's part led to the bombshell testimony of the Watergate Committee hearing.

Sanders met privately with Alexander Butterfield, a former special assistant to the president, whose job had been to maintain a log of notes and memoranda related to staff conversations with the president. Acting on his hunch, Sanders asked Butterfield, "Do you know of any basis for the implication in John Dean's testimony that conversations in the Oval Office are recorded?"[17]

After hesitating for a moment, Butterfield replied, "Well, I was afraid you might ask me that question."

Butterfield disclosed that a recording system had been installed in the Oval Office. Incredibly, most of the president's conversations in the Oval Office had been recorded, and the tapes still existed.

Don Sanders shared the news with Fred Thompson, who then shared the news with Senator Baker.[18] Their initial reaction was that this was good news for the president. Baker thought it "inconceivable" that Nixon would have taped his conversations if they contained anything incriminating.

Thompson agreed. In fact, Thompson considered the possibility that "Butterfield had been sent to us as part of a strategy. The president was orchestrating the whole affair and had intended that the tapes be discovered. Then he would produce the tapes, or perhaps play them publicly; there would be nothing incriminating, and John Dean's testimony would be utterly discredited."

They called Butterfield to testify publicly before the committee.

On Monday morning, July 16, Butterfield appeared, and was questioned by Thompson.[19]

"Mr. Butterfield," the minority counsel inquired, "Are you aware of the installation of any listening devices in the Oval Office of the president?"

The Senate Caucus Room grew silent.

"I was aware of listening devices. Yes, sir," Butterfield responded.

He testified that listening devices had been installed in the Oval Office, the Executive Office Building, and the Cabinet Room. There were also listening devices on the telephones in the Lincoln Room and in the president's office at Camp David.

Thompson continued his examination. "And as far as you know, those tapes are still available?"

"As far as I know," Butterfield said, "but I've been away for four months, sir."

Everyone in the Senate Caucus Room and millions watching on television realized that one of two things was true. Either the tapes were still in existence, or they had been destroyed after the creation of the Watergate Committee.

If the tapes still existed, there would be a clear and definitive answer to Senator Howard Baker's question: "What did the president know, and when did he know it?"

The answer was not immediately forthcoming. To the surprise of Senator Baker and Fred Thompson, the White House conceded that the tapes existed—but would not voluntarily produce the relevant tapes, providing only incomplete transcripts.

This in turn led to a series of events that Senator Ervin would call "the greatest constitutional crisis since the Civil War."

On Saturday evening, October 20, 1973, the president instructed Attorney General Elliot Richardson to fire the special prosecutor,

Archibald Cox. Richardson refused and resigned in protest, explaining that he had promised to back Cox's independence.

The president then ordered Deputy Attorney General William Ruckelshaus to fire Archibald Cox. Ruckelshaus also refused and resigned in protest, claiming that he too had promised to back the independence of the special prosecutor.

The president then contacted the solicitor general of the United States, Robert Bork, and ordered him to fire the special prosecutor. Bork did so, having made no promises to the special prosecutor and having been encouraged by both Richardson and Ruckelshaus to stay in his position in the Justice Department. The events of that evening ignited a firestorm that would go down in history as "the Saturday Night Massacre."

In an effort to get the tapes, two lawsuits were then filed against the president, one by the Watergate committee, and one by the special prosecutor.

On July 24, 1974, after months of legal battles, the United States Supreme Court issued a unanimous 8-0 decision in the case of *United States v. Nixon*. The Court rejected the president's claim that he had absolute immunity from judicial process. The Watergate tapes had to be released to the special prosecutor.

When the tapes were released on August 8, 1974, the nation got an immediate, clear, and unequivocal answer to Senator Baker's question. The transcripts of the conversation of June 23, 1972, between H.R. Haldeman and President Nixon revealed that the president had ordered that the FBI be directed to pull away from the Watergate matter.

When the news came, Fred Thompson found Senator Baker in a committee meeting. The senator stepped out of the room to talk with him.[20]

"Well, I guess this is finally it, isn't it?" Thompson asked.

"Yes," Senator Baker replied. "And it's time. He will be gone by the end of the week."

Baker took no joy in what had happened. In fact, he had agonized over the events.

The Watergate hearings had been the greatest challenge of Baker's public career. But he had responded to that challenge.

Years later, Senator Fred Thompson would look back on the Watergate hearings as "the last bipartisan investigation we've had."[21] The Iran-Contra hearings in the 1980s and the impeachment of President Clinton in the 1990s were both partisan investigations, with Democrats on one side and Republicans on the other.

But in the spring of 1973, Senator Howard Baker, a Republican, had sat beside Senator Sam Ervin, a Democrat, in the Senate Caucus Room. They were two bright country lawyers who worked together to respond to the greatest constitutional crisis since the Civil War.

Senator Baker, shutterbug. Reprinted with the permission of Senator Baker and the Baker Center.

*"When I leave this mortal coil, I may have no money.
I may have no reputation,
but I'll have a lot of good pictures."*

—*Howard Baker Jr.*

CHAPTER 13

An Eloquent Observer

On October 8, 1974, President Gerald Ford was in the lobby of the Knoxville Hyatt Regency Hotel on his way to give a speech to an economic development conference.

Secret service agents sighted a short man with several cameras dangling around his neck following the president.

In the agents' professional opinion, the man was following the president way too closely.

The agents quickly intervened, took the man by the arm, and escorted him to a roped-off area. The man did not object. He just kept snapping photographs of the president. To the alarm of the secret service agents, the man then slipped under the rope and dashed back to the side of the president. The secret service agents were about to take the man into custody when they noticed the president smiling and talking with him.

To their embarrassment, the agents discovered that the man with the cameras was the senior senator from Tennessee.[1]

Years later, dozens of reporters clustered around Senator Baker's office in the Capitol after midnight, awaiting word from a meeting in Baker's office over a deadlock in a budget fight. Suddenly, the office door opened and Baker emerged. The reporters went silent, awaiting an announcement. The senator said nothing. He pointed his cameras at the reporters and took several photos.[2]

"I got some great pictures," the senator said proudly, and then went back in his office.

On that autumn day in Knoxville and that late night at the Capitol, Baker was happily engaging in his avocation, photography.

Baker took his first photograph in 1937 at the age of twelve, developing it in a darkroom he had made at his home in Huntsville.[3]

From that point on, at least one camera and often two (a Hasselblad and an R3 Leica) dangled from his neck almost every day of his life.[4] The senator once estimated that he had taken and developed more than a quarter of a million photographs. Those photographs had constituted his pictorial diary.

"A lot of people write diaries—keep diaries and day books—but this is a record of my life. This is my diary, my recollection of campaigns and other times as well," Baker said.

During his years in the Senate, Baker's refuge was always his darkroom.[5] Staffers remember that when he needed to unwind or simply have some personal time to reflect on a difficult decision, he would abruptly leave his office in the Capitol and head for home. There he would retreat into his darkroom.

The senator's daughter, Cissy, remembers that on most evenings when her father would return to their Washington home, he would go first to his darkroom. He would spend a few solitary moments developing photographs, before emerging to have dinner with Cissy, her brother Darek, and her mother.[6]

Baker would sometimes interrupt meetings in the Capitol to take a call from a photography supply store.[7] His aides would hear him happily lost in a discussion of "cosine errors" or "density channels."

Baker also used his photography as a tool in his work as a Senate leader. In 1979, as Senate minority leader, Baker dispatched

Senator John Danforth to fly to Cambodia on a fact-finding mission regarding the terrible mass starvation that plagued that country.[8]

"You should take a camera and take lots of pictures of what you see," Baker told him.

Baker also instructed Danforth on how to take the pictures.

"He said it was very important to get close to the subjects and isolate them as individuals," Danforth remembered.[9]

Danforth turned out to be a very good photography student. When he returned from Cambodia and shared his pictures with the minority leader, Baker was so impressed that he arranged for the photos to be presented as a slide show to President Carter in the White House Cabinet Room. On the following day, Senator Danforth testified before the Senate Foreign Relations Committee, again presenting the slides of his compelling photographs.

That evening, Dan Rather showed the pictures on the *CBS Evening News*.[10]

"As a result," Senator Danforth later wrote, "what had been an obscure story of suffering in Cambodia became national news."

The American people responded with an outpouring of contributions to the Red Cross, and Congress passed a $30 million emergency supplemental appropriation for humanitarian assistance to the Cambodians.

Danforth was not the only Senate member tasked with photography. The minority leader asked other senators to document their investigations with photographs. For Baker, photographs were an essential part of congressional fact-finding.

When he would return home to Tennessee, the senator would spend hours photographing the mountains and streams of Big South Fork Country. Most of all, he loved to take photographs of his fellow ordinary Tennesseans. Congressman Bill Jenkins recalls how on one occasion, the senator was late for a speech because he was in a blacksmith's shop photographing one of his constituents hard at work.[11]

In the introduction to *Howard Baker's Washington*, a 1982 collection of his photographs, the senator described his avocation:

> I'm a fortunate man in many ways, but I'm most fortunate in having a hobby that has stayed with me all my life. It's a great saving grace. It permits me to relieve my anxiety and to escape from the frustrations or the disappointments or even the exhilaration of the moment. Photography gives me the opportunity to re-establish fresh perspectives. It gives me an outlet for whatever creative energy I have, and it gives me a record of my life. And that may be the most important value of all. [12]

The senator's love of photography was a reflection of his civility.[13] Just as he was an eloquent listener, he was also an eloquent observer.

"There are two tracks in my personality," he said. "One of them tries hard to do my job. The other runs along more or less parallel, sort of watching what's going on."

Baker long denied that politics was his first love and photography was his hobby.

"The facts are just the opposite," he said. "When I leave this mortal coil, I may have no money. I may have no reputation, but I'll have a lot of good pictures." [14]

CHAPTER 14

Saving the Panama Canal

On September 4, 1977, a full-page ad appeared in the *Tennessean* featuring a bold headline: "Senator Baker alone can save the Panama Canal."[1]

When he saw the ad, Howard Baker responded with both consternation and self-deprecating humor. "It never dawned on me that only I could save the Panama Canal," he deadpanned to his Senate colleagues.[2]

The ad urged readers to "write, call, or visit" the senator.

"Which one do you think they will do?" Joy Baker asked.

"Probably all three," her husband replied.[3]

Later that fall, Howard and Joy Baker were sitting in Knoxville's Neyland Stadium, part of a crowd over 100,000, watching the Tennessee Volunteers play an SEC foe. At halftime, a plane flew over the stadium. Attached to the back of the plane was a streaming banner that read:

"Senator Baker, save the Panama Canal!"[4]

The *Tennessean* ad had been paid for by the American Conservative Union. The airplane had been rented by the University of Tennessee chapter of the Young Americans for Freedom.

Suddenly, Baker found himself at the epicenter of a political storm: The proposed Senate ratification of the Torrijos-Carter Treaties, better known as "the Panama Canal Treaty."

In 1903, President Theodore Roosevelt had dispatched the gunboat *Nashville* to help the Panamanian people earn their independence from Columbia.[5] Thereafter, the United States had secured a treaty giving it the exclusive rights to build a canal through the Isthmus of Panama and to control it "in perpetuity." Over the next ten years, the United States spent $375 million in construction of the canal, the single most expensive construction project in American history to that time.

Beginning in 1914, over a thousand American ships passed each day from the Atlantic to the Pacific through the canal.

But by the 1960s, US control of the canal had become the source of resentment by the Panamanian people.[6] And by the 1970s, the canal had become the focal point of anti-American sentiment throughout Latin America.

General Omar Torrijos had come to power in Panama in a 1968 coup. Torrijos maintained his power by demanding a new "just and fair" treaty that would "guarantee full respect for Panama's effective sovereignty."

The administrations of Presidents Johnson, Nixon, and Ford had tried unsuccessfully to deal with the issue, but they had only succeeded in buying time.

By 1977, it was clear that if a new agreement between the two countries was not reached, violence would strike, endangering American interests in Panama and throughout Latin America.[7]

In 1977, President Jimmy Carter dealt with the issue head-on, negotiating the Torrijos-Carter treaties, which stipulated that the Panama Canal would be formally handed over to Panama on December 31, 1999.[8] The issue then went to the US Senate, where the treaties had to be ratified by a two-thirds majority.

President Jimmy Carter and Senator Baker. Reprinted with the permission of Senator Baker and the Baker Center.

The result was a political firestorm and an "unwelcome challenge" for the Senate minority leader, Howard Baker.[9]

During a Senate recess in August 1977, Baker was back in Tennessee. He was enjoying time with his family and traveling the state in anticipation of his 1978 re-election campaign. His working vacation was interrupted by a call from the White House.

A few months later, in a speech to the Senate, Baker took the liberty of recalling the phone conversation:

> The president came on the line to tell me that negotiations with Panama were about complete, and that he wanted me to know of this in advance.
>
> The president also said that he hoped that the treaty could be submitted to the Senate

immediately, and that we could have early action on that treaty in 1977.

I'm sure the president will not be offended if I repeat now my reply in substance. I try to make it a policy not to repeat conversations in which only presidents and I are present, but I think this is important, and I believe the president would not judge it inappropriate to deviate from that personal policy. I thought for a minute and replied:

Mr. President, I'm sure you know as certainly as I know that this is an issue that will generate strong emotions, that will divide my state, the country, and indeed divide my party and your party, too.

One only has to recall that extraordinary contest in the Republican Presidential Primary in 1976 when this was certainly one of the principle issues in the campaign between President Ford and Governor Reagan, to know that it is going to be divisive. It is going to be difficult. And I must say, Mr. President, that I want you to know that I will consciously make the decision not to decide how I will vote during this year, and I will wait until the first of January to make that determination, because I want to make certain that I fulfill my responsibilities as a senator to my state and as minority leader to my party in the Senate.

The senator would later more informally recall, "I wish he (the president) hadn't asked (for my support). This had been kicking around for years. (I wondered) why now, and why me?"

Facing a re-election campaign in 1978, Baker heard from his constituents in Tennessee.[10]

The message was overwhelming and clear. By mid-March of

1978, the senator had received 64,000 letters, almost all urging him to vote against the treaties. Typical was a letter he received from a constituent in Knoxville:

> Are your constituents from Tennessee—who vote for you and have written you concerning this matter—so dumb, ignorant, and illiterate that our opinions are of no significance, or will our senator feed us what is good for us and ignore our opinions? See you at the ballot box!

As the senator wryly observed at the time, "advice and views were never in short supply."

Governor Ronald Reagan was already launching his 1980 presidential campaign, making his opposition to the Panama Canal Treaty a centerpiece. The Great Communicator said unequivocally that the ratification of the Panama Canal Treaty, would be "the greatest mistake in American history."[11]

Senator Baker's friends and supporters in Tennessee warned him of the adverse political consequences if he supported the treaty. During a trip home to Huntsville, Baker was enjoying a game of tennis with his friend, Bill Swain. Between sets, Swain brought up the subject of the canal, half-kiddingly saying that he, like most Tennesseans, agreed with Senator S.I. Hayakawa: "We stole the canal fair and square, and we should keep it!"[12]

Baker was not amused, and he responded with a brief epithet. It is one of the few times Swain had ever heard his friend curse.

Throughout the fall of 1977 and into the winter of 1978, Baker's civility and collegiality faced its greatest test.

True to form, the senator did not know at the outset whether he would support the treaties' ratification. The easy and politically expedient course would have been to oppose the treaties. This would have guaranteed him a landslide victory in Tennessee in 1978 and perhaps made him the front-runner for the GOP presidential nomination in 1980.

But like his father-in-law, Baker was not going to oppose a treaty simply because it had been proposed by a Democratic president. In 1963, Senator Everett Dirksen had been criticized for supporting President Kennedy's proposed Nuclear Test Ban Treaty. Dirksen's response was, "He's my president, too."

Baker regarded the situation in Panama as a very complex issue that merited a thoughtful response. He soon made it clear to the voters in Tennessee and throughout America that he was not going to yield to party politics or emotion on the issue. He had a duty as leader of the US Senate, and he intended to fulfill it.

Baker would do what he had done during his eighteen years as a lawyer and his ten previous years in the Senate. He would do what he had done during the Watergate investigation and in response to every other challenging issue he had faced.

First, he would become completely informed by the interests of both sides of the issue, foregoing influence by either the media or his own political party.[13] The senator commissioned two consultants, both leading experts in US-Latin American relations. One was an advocate for the treaties, and the other was against them. Just as he had done with competing lobbyists on previous issues, the senator worked with both in gathering all available information underlying the proposed treaties.

In January of 1978, the senator led a fact-finding mission to Panama "to see first-hand Panama and the internal arrangements, meaning Torrijos and his governance, and to give other senators an opportunity to see what the circumstances were."[14]

The trip was highly criticized, characterized in one newspaper editorial as "an expensive decision" that was being funded by American taxpayers.

As he had with so many issues in his career, Baker asked questions, listened, and gathered information.

He concluded that the treaties needed to be ratified, to stabilize the situation in Panama and Latin America and to protect American interests. He also felt that the treaties needed amendments, not only to secure Senate ratification but also to guarantee America's "right to an open and secure passageway connecting the planet's two principal oceans, and the proper means to insure it."[15]

Baker joined forces with his friend, Senator Robert Byrd, in a bipartisan effort to secure ratification.

Baker and Byrd proposed two amendments that expressed in clear and unequivocal language both the canal's neutrality and America's position pursuant to the neutrality treaty.[16]

The first amendment declared, "The provisions of this article shall not be construed as conferring upon the United States of America a right of intervention in the internal affairs of the Republic of Panama, and any action by the United States of America pursuant to this article shall not be directed against the territorial integrity or political independence of the Republic of Panama."

The second amendment guaranteed US ships priority during times of need, allowing them to go to the head of the canal line without delay.

Senator Dennis DeConcini then proposed a third amendment, proclaiming that the United States would have the right to "take such steps as it deems necessary, including force, to re-open the canal or restore operations of the canal."

Baker then became the leading advocate for the amendments, requiring him to convince not only his fellow senators, but also President Carter and General Torrijos.

Accompanied by a dozen senators, Baker told President Carter that there was no way the Senate would consent to the treaties unless the amendments passed, securing the US right to defend the canal and have priority passage for American ships.[17]

The senator then met personally with General Torrijos in Panama. He gave the general a reality check. He told him that the treaties would never be ratified by the Senate without the proposed amendments.

"There can be no doubt about our rights to use force to protect the canal," Baker told him. "And in time of emergency, our Navy ships have to be able to get through the canal as fast as possible."[18]

Torrijos relented, provided that there would be no further amendments that would require the general to resubmit the treaty to another Panamanian plebiscite for approval.

Dealing with the senator's Republican colleagues, however, was a taller order. Fourteen Republican Congressmen publicly called for Baker to back down: "We respectfully suggest that (the senator) formally step aside as the minority leader of the Senate for the duration of the debate on the Panama Canal Treaties."

Baker stood firm, with continued strategic civility. He freely acknowledged that a number of his Republican colleagues would have to oppose ratification of the treaties, but said that his support would provide appropriate "cover" for other Republicans whose votes would be needed to secure the two-thirds majority vote. Baker stated simply that this was "part of my role as minority leader."

On March 16, 1978, the United States Senate voted 68-32 to ratify the first treaty, the so-called Neutrality Treaty.[19]

On April 15, 1978, the Senate cast the same vote, 68-32, in support of the second treaty designed to secure American interests.

Both treaties had passed with just one vote to spare.

Just months after the treaties were ratified, Baker was back in Tennessee. He found himself in a surprisingly tough fight for re-election to a third term.

His Democratic opponent Jane Eskind, a former liberal, had become a born-again conservative. She ran ads against the senator, blasting him for "giving away the Panama Canal."

"What is best for the country must always take precedence," Baker responded.[20]

The senator was re-elected.

However, in his 1980 presidential campaign, his support of the Panama Canal Treaties surfaced again. To this day, Baker's closest friends believe his support of the treaties cost him the presidency.

But the senator's bipartisan efforts in the fall of 1977 and in the winter of 1978 had in fact transformed the relationship of the United States and Panama, stabilized the situation in Latin America, and guaranteed protection of American interests in the canal.

Ironically, the full page ad that appeared in the *Tennessean* and the banner that flew over the football stadium both proved to be correct. Senator Baker had saved the Panama Canal.

Senator Baker campaigning for the presidency, 1980. Reprinted with the permission of Senator Baker and the Baker Center.

"I constantly tried to persuade Howard that it was important for him to clearly articulate why he wanted to be president. In fact, I made myself something of a pest by repeatedly asking that question."

—*Senator John Danforth*

CHAPTER 15

The Unmaking of the President, 1980

Tom Griscom remembers the moment the 1980 Baker for President Campaign ended, for all intents and purposes. It did not happen on the last day of the campaign.

It happened on one of the first.

On the night of January 4, 1980, Baker and Griscom, his press secretary, boarded the senator's private plane, the de Havilland Sky Hawker. Baker's longtime friend and pilot, Lonnie Strunk, was left seat, the senator right. They departed Washington National Airport and headed for Iowa, where the senator would begin his campaign to win the Iowa Caucus and get a jump start toward the Republican presidential nomination.[1]

But when Baker landed in Des Moines, there was big news awaiting him. Shortly after Baker, his press secretary, and his buddy, Lonnie, were wheels up, President Jimmy Carter had announced he was imposing a grain embargo on the Soviet Union.[2]

It was a huge news story, particularly in Iowa, the nation's leading corn-producing state. The embargo would immediately become the biggest issue in the Republican Iowa Caucus. As soon as Senator Baker climbed out of his plane and walked into Des Moines airport, he was greeted by Tom Pettit of *NBC News*. With the camera rolling, Pettit asked the senator, "What do you think about President Carter's grain embargo?"[3]

It did not take a political genius with overnight tracking polls to know how that question should be answered if you wanted to win the Iowa Caucus. But Baker didn't hesitate.

"Tom, I really can't take a position until I talk to the president to understand what he is doing on all this," the senator said.

Standing beside his boss, Griscom felt in his bones "the whole presidential campaign going down the proverbial tube."[4]

The response was vintage Howard Baker. Thoughtful. Civil. It was the response of a man who was a senator first and a candidate second. It was the response of a man who, like his father-in-law before him, was not going to automatically oppose a president's position, even if the president was from a rival political party and was someone whose job Baker was trying to take.

Griscom, the veteran political reporter, understood that the senator's response was not what Iowa voters wanted to hear.

Ronald Reagan, George Bush, and other GOP candidates in the Caucus made it clear to the Iowa voters that, unlike Senator Baker, they did not need to talk with President Carter to understand why the grain embargo had been imposed. They thought it was a terrible idea, and they were against it.

Senator John Danforth was one of the first Republicans who got on board the Baker for President bandwagon, but he was concerned that his friend had a major weakness as a presidential candidate.

"Howard was the most modest and self-effacing politician I ever met in my life," Danforth said. "And he couldn't answer the Roger Mudd question."[5]

That was a reference to a very simple question that Mudd, a CBS reporter, had asked Senator Edward Kennedy on a *60 Minutes* segment in the fall of 1979: "Why do you want to be president?"

Kennedy had stumbled badly in his response. Danforth felt his friend would have the same problem on the campaign trail.

"I constantly tried to persuade Howard that it was important for him to clearly articulate why he wanted to be president," Danforth said. "In fact, I made myself something of a pest by repeatedly asking that question. I do believe that (Howard's) inability to give a clear answer was related to his character, which is the opposite of being messianic."[6]

Baker placed a distant third in the Iowa Caucus, with fifteen percent of the vote, compared to thirty-two percent for George Bush and thirty percent for Ronald Reagan.

Baker's presidential campaign would move on to primaries in New Hampshire, Maine, and Massachusetts. But it soon became clear that Baker the presidential candidate had two liabilities. First, he had a full-time job as minority leader of the Senate. His job took time away from his time on the campaign trail, and as the grain embargo issue demonstrated, it placed restraints on his campaign positions. Baker was a Senator first and a presidential candidate second.

Baker lamented that "maybe you have to be unemployed to run for president." In fact, his chief political adviser, Doug Bailey, urged him to resign from the Senate and devote himself full-time to the campaign, but Baker would not even consider the idea.

"How," he asked, "am I going to explain to all those folks who elected me to the Senate, and then I resign?"

Baker's second liability was his bipartisanship. It wasn't just his position on the Panama Canal. The centerpiece of his campaign was bipartisanship. He told Republican primary voters in New Hampshire and Maine and Massachusetts that he would reach out to not only Republicans, but to Democrats and independents just as he had in Tennessee, contending that that's what made him the strongest Republican candidate against President Carter.

But presidential primaries are by definition *partisan* events, and a speech about bipartisanship was not exactly a crowd-pleaser.

Throughout his brief campaign, Baker also talked about a very civil idea. He noted that President Jimmy Carter had begun his presidency with a symbolic act. In January 1977, immediately after his inauguration, he had walked up Pennsylvania Avenue from the Capitol to the White House.

Baker promised that if he was elected president, he would begin his administration with a different symbolic act. He would conclude the inaugural ceremony by opening a presidential office in the Capitol itself, where he could deal daily and personally with the men and women who enacted the laws of the land.[7]

It was the campaign promise of a man who had a clear knowledge of how Washington worked, or how it should work. But it was not an idea that would win the hearts and minds of Republican primary voters.

Years later, Baker's friend, Congressman Morris Udall, would write *Too Funny to Be President*, a memoir about his own unsuccessful presidential campaign in 1976. If there had been a memoir about Baker's campaign, it might have been *Too Civil to Be President*.

After successive defeats in primaries in New Hampshire, Maine, and Massachusetts, Baker assessed his campaign. The columnist Hugh Sidey summarized it for readers of the *Washington Star*: "(Baker) figured out that he had been through 43 states, 347 counties, 155 and a half Holiday Inns, three of Arthur Adler's best suits, 197 chicken wings, and 1,324 Rolaids."[8]

Baker made another calculation. He figured out that he "drank more cans of Tab while campaigning than he had gotten votes."

As Hugh Sidey concluded, "Senator Baker got the message, from his alimentary canal, if no other place."

Baker was fond of saying that his primary job as a Senate leader was to "count carefully, and often."

Baker had counted the votes and the delegates, and in his own frank words, he concluded, "It is clear that my campaign was not going anywhere."[9]

Baker suspended his campaign and returned to Washington.

But there was one group who did not vote in any of the Republican primaries in 1980. Had they been the voters, the outcome of the civil campaign of Howard Baker for President might have been dramatically different. *Newsweek* asked a sample of Democratic senators off the record who they would like to see elected president in 1980. A *Newsweek* reporter confidentially told a Senate Democrat that a plurality of his Senate colleagues backed Baker.

"You're wrong," the Democrat replied. "He would win a majority."[10]

Senator Baker in the majority leader's office. Reprinted with the permission of Senator Baker and the Baker Center.

CHAPTER 16

A New Office Does Not Require a New Office

Early on Wednesday, November 5, 1980, Senator Howard Baker placed a phone call to his friend and Senate colleague, Paul Laxalt of Nevada.[1]

Just a few hours earlier, Ronald Wilson Reagan had swept to a landslide victory over President Jimmy Carter, carrying forty-three states and winning the Electoral College by a margin of 489-49.[2] Republicans had also won formerly Democrat Senate seats in Alabama, Idaho, Iowa, North Carolina, Wisconsin, and Georgia. For the first time since 1954, Republicans had gained control of the Senate. In just four years, Republicans had gone from just thirty-eight Senate members to fifty-three.

Baker placed his early morning call to Paul Laxalt because Laxalt was more than a fellow senator. He just happened to be President-Elect Reagan's closest friend in the US Senate.

On election night, when Baker realized that his party would take control of the Senate, he knew that it was not a foregone conclusion that he would now move from minority leader to majority leader.

Baker sensed that his conservative Republican colleagues—and particularly the "freshman class" of Republican senators just elected—would be looking to continue the Reagan Revolution by electing a majority leader with unquestionable conservative credentials. That candidate would most likely be Paul Laxalt, Baker realized.

And so when the senior senator from Tennessee reached the senior senator from Nevada by phone early in the morning after the historic election, he asked for a favor: Would Laxalt nominate him as majority leader?[3]

Without hesitation, Laxalt enthusiastically agreed.

Over the next few weeks, there was a concerted effort by some "New Right" political leaders to find a conservative alternative to Baker as majority leader.

But Paul Laxalt and his fellow Republican conservative senators such as Charles Grassley, James Abdnor, Dan Quayle, and notably, Bob Dole, had seen first-hand Howard Baker's style as minority leader, and they now felt that same approach was necessary in the Republican majority leader.

Senator Dole in particular sensed that the new president's conservative agenda could easily get bogged down in bitter ideological fights with liberal Democrats in the Senate. Dole was a conservative, but he was also a practical politician, and he knew that for the Reagan Revolution to succeed, the new president would need a Senate majority leader who was trusted on both sides of the aisle and who was a master at building consensus. Baker was that man, Dole realized.

Significantly, another person who realized Baker was the right man for the job was the president-elect, Ronald Reagan.

Even before inauguration day, Baker established a good working relationship with the incoming Reagan White House. While

Baker had opposed Reagan in the primaries of 1980, Reagan respected the civil tone of Baker's campaign. The new president recognized that Baker had the temperament and demeanor to be his leader in the Senate.

When the 97th session of the US Congress convened on January 3, 1981, Baker was unanimously elected majority leader.

Four years earlier, on his first day as minority leader, the senator had reached out to his opposition leader, Bob Byrd. And now, in his first act as majority leader, he would do so again.

For four years, Byrd had occupied the large corner office Capitol suite that had long been the offices of the Senate majority leader. In the 1950s, Lyndon Johnson had wielded power over the Senate in these impressive offices that were so large and palatial that they became known to senators as "Taj Mahal."

"This is the second best view in Washington," Baker said of his office overlooking the Mall. "Only the Rose Garden from the Oval Office tops it."

Baker was expected to move from S-231 to Taj Mahal. But with Baker, a new office did not require a new office.

Baker met with his old friend, Bob Byrd, and told him there was no need to swap offices. Senator Byrd could remain in Taj Mahal, and Senator Baker would happily remain in S-231.[4]

The truth of the matter was that Baker absolutely loved S-231 and did not want to leave it. He loved the history of the oldest occupied office in the Capitol. He loved the view from his office window, looking down on the Mall and the monuments and the hills of Arlington.

"This is the second best view in Washington," he told the *Washington Post*'s David Broder. "Only the Rose Garden from the Oval Office tops it."[5]

The senator also loved working in the office where his father-in-law, Everett Dirksen, had worked as the minority leader from

1959 to 1969. He particularly enjoyed showing visitors the fireplace by his desk.[6] He would tell them that during the years his father-in-law had served as minority leader, Senator Dirksen would often complain that the fireplace did not work, claiming it had been sealed years earlier when the Capitol had been air-conditioned.

Senator Baker had accepted his father-in-law's words at face value. After Baker had moved into S-231 in 1977 as minority leader, he asked a Capitol maintenance man what it would take to put that fireplace into service.

"Well, some kindling and a match, I suppose," the maintenance man responded.

The fireplace had never been sealed.

Baker would laugh and say that that was the only time he had ever known his father-in-law to be wrong.

Baker was especially fond of an old mahogany table that sat in S-231. Some of the most significant decisions in American history had been made around that conference table. Senator Dirksen had hammered out the agreement on the Civil Rights Act of 1964 on that table. More recently, the agreement concerning the Panama Canal Treaties had been reached on the old mahogany table.[7]

Senator Baker could have moved the table into Taj Mahal, but he wanted it to stay right there in S-231. And he wanted to stay there as well.

Unbeknownst to his Senate colleagues, the senator had a wonderful plan to renovate the conference room of S-231 that had housed the original Library of Congress.[8] The 3,000 volumes that were once on its shelves had been burned by the British when they torched the Capitol in 1814. But the titles of the books were known and cataloged in the Library of Congress. Baker planned to raise a million dollars in private contributions to have copies of the 3,000 books rebound and placed in the original bookshelves in S-231.

Of course, Howard Baker didn't tell Bob Byrd any of this. He simply told him there was no need to swap offices. It was an act of civility by Senator Howard Baker. But once again, it was an act of *strategic* civility.

Baker's next act as majority leader was also civil, bipartisan, and as it turned out, controversial. With the return to power for the first time in twenty-six years, the Republican Senate leadership was entitled to dismiss scores of Democrat Senate staff members. To the victors belonged the spoils.

But Baker did not want to lose the talent, skills, and experience of many staffers simply because they were Democrats.[9]

With the new Republican majority, two-thirds of the Senate staffers would be hired by Republican Senators, and one-third by Democrats.

Senator Baker let it be known that he hoped that many experienced Democratic staffers would be retained.[10]

The senator's recommendation was not well-received by a number of his Republican colleagues. He dismissed the criticism.

"We're in charge, and we're going to make sure we have a majority so we can manage the process," he said. "But we're not going to lose the skills that come with years of experience from the Democrats just because we're in charge and they're not."[11]

> *"We're not going to lose the skills that come with years of experience from the Democrats just because we're in charge and they're not."*
>
> —*Senator Baker*

The senator's press secretary, Tom Griscom, regarded this decision as vintage Baker strategic civility.

"Civility is understanding what you are trying to get done," Griscom explained. "Experience is what you need to be able to make it happen. Anybody that watches the Senate knows how the process works. Staff is important. Staff is where the activity goes on and where a lot of melding occurs. You have to have a staff that's smart, and you have to trust them. You don't just get rid of all the experienced ones because you've taken over. That's when you can make mistakes."[12]

Having saved Senator Byrd's Taj Mahal and several Democratic staffers their jobs, the new majority leader turned his attention to his fifty-two fellow Republican senators. Bringing them together and keeping them together shaped up as an even bigger challenge than obtaining bipartisan support from Senator Byrd and the Democrats.

The Senate's freshman Class of 1980 included conservative ideologues, including Alfonse D'Amato of New York, Charles Grassley of Iowa, and Mack Mattingly of Georgia. But the Republican side of the Senate aisle also included liberals like Mark Hatfield of Oregon and Lowell Weicker of Connecticut. Trying to assemble such an eclectic group as a united front was, to use Baker's favorite analogy, "like herding cats."

In the first week of the 97th Congress, Senator Baker reached out to the twelve freshman Republican senators, setting up weekly lunches in rotating groups of four.[13] The lunches would be held in the majority leader's office, and at the end of each lunch, Baker would get on his "hot line" to the White House. With the freshman senators sitting beside or across from him around the old mahogany table, the majority leader would talk directly to Max L. Friedersdorf, President Reagan's congressional liaison, and would share with him the views, insights, or requests from the new senators. The message to the freshmen was clear: You are not expected to be seen and not heard. The majority leader wants your input, and he wants it now.

Baker then set up weekly meetings with the Republican committee chairmen to go over the agendas of their respective committees. One freshman senator from a rotating roster would also be invited to sit in on these weekly meetings, and other interested senators would be invited as well.[14]

Baker would lead these meetings to accomplish two purposes.

First, it gave him as majority leader "a central role in managing the flow of legislation."

Second, it gave all the committee chairmen an overview of the agenda, too.

The result, as columnist David Broder would observe, was "a sense of teamwork among Republican senators of diverse views."

That teamwork was soon necessary when President Reagan and his Senate majority leader faced the first legislative challenge of the new administration.

The federal debt limit had to be raised to one trillion dollars.

It was a distasteful task, but something that had to be done to avoid a shutdown of the federal government.

All twelve freshman Republican senators told the new majority leader they could not support raising the debt limit. They had just been elected campaigning against such a proposal. In addition, a large number of veteran Republican senators had never voted to increase the debt ceiling and were reluctant to do so even with Ronald Reagan in the White House.[15]

Baker knew there was one Republican in the Senate who could lead and win the fight to raise the federal debt ceiling. He was also the least likely member of the Senate to do so.[16]

But Baker went to Senator Strom Thurmond and convinced the Senate's most conservative member—a man who for decades had railed against raising the federal debt ceiling—that he had to lead this fight in support of President Reagan.

The majority leader then summoned the twelve Republican freshmen to his office, where they gathered around the old mahogany table. Thurmond then walked into the room and spoke to the freshman class.[17]

"Gentlemen, I understand your concern that you have always opposed an increase in the debt limit. Some of you served in the House, and you have never voted to increase it. Well, neither have I. But I've never had Ronald Reagan as president before, so I'm going to vote for it, and I believe you should, too," Thurmond said.

"It was a damned effective speech," Baker later recalled.[18]

A lot of eyebrows were raised in the Capitol when word got out about the meeting and people realized that Senator Strom Thurmond, of all people, was leading the fight to raise the federal debt ceiling to a trillion dollars.

But *NBC News* Chief Congressional Correspondent Lisa Myers was not surprised. She never underestimated Baker's power to build unlikely coalitions.

"That man can bring a boll weevil and a cotton planter together," she observed.

Having succeeded in raising the federal debt ceiling, the new majority leader turned his attention to forging bipartisan coalitions in support of President Reagan's two most controversial proposals—tax and budget cuts.

On August 31, 1981, President Reagan interrupted a vacation at his Santa Barbara ranch to sign two bills into law. The first cut marginal tax rates by five percent as of October 1981, ten percent in 1982, and ten percent in 1983. The other bill cut 35.1 billion dollars in spending from the fiscal 1982 budget.[19]

> *"That man can bring a boll weevil and a cotton planter together."*
>
> —Lisa Myers

It was a triumph for the president. It had come about due to the bipartisan leadership of the Senate majority leader.

The *New York Times* called President Reagan's first few months in office "the most dramatic first 100 days since FDR."[20]

Over the next four years, Baker's reputation grew as the most successful majority leader since Lyndon B. Johnson. But while LBJ had ruled the Senate from Taj Mahal as a ruthless power broker, Baker took a different approach on the Senate floor and at his desk by the now-working fireplace in S-231. He was patient, unfailingly polite, and respectful of the views of all one hundred senators.

"He was a master of friendly persuasion, whose warm and reasonable way could bring senators to his point of view," John Danforth said. "He had strength without belligerence."[21]

His leadership style, *The Almanac of American Politics* would note, was "more readily adaptable to television and to the temperament to deal easily with his colleagues."[22]

Time after time, at the end of heated debates, he would find a path to compromise—often to the surprise of his fellow senators.

On one occasion after getting the full Baker treatment around the old mahogany desk, Senators Jesse Helms and Lowell Weicker left S-231 bewildered that the majority leader had convinced them to agree on an issue. As they walked down the Capitol hallway together, the liberal Weicker turned to the conservative Helms and said, "I'm not sure what just happened. You know one of us is dead wrong."

Years later, during his own era as majority leader, Senator Trent Lott would recall Baker's leadership style:

> There is nothing in any political science textbook that explains the unique way Baker led the Senate. But those who were part of it at the time remember. They remember his coolness and his patience, even under personal attack.
>
> They remembered how, seemingly nonchalant, he would let policy battles rage for days on the Senate floor, with all senators fully exercising their right to debate. And then, when the voices calmed and the tempers died down, there would be an informal gathering in his office.
>
> After a while, the anxious staffers outside would hear laughter, probably the result of an anecdote aptly timed to break the ice and bring about a civil consensus.[23]

Howard Baker's leadership style was admired not just by his Republican colleagues. As the 97th Congress drew to a close, the new minority leader, Robert Byrd, remarked on it.

"President Reagan should thank his lucky stars every day that he has Howard Baker here as majority leader," Byrd said.

At the other end of Pennsylvania Avenue, the president of the United States was indeed thankful for his majority leader.

He told his advisers, "I am frank to say that I don't think we could have had the successes we've had . . . without (Howard Baker's) leadership."

CHAPTER 17

A Rose for Mrs. Packwood

Early in his tenure as majority leader, Senator Howard Baker faced what would be his toughest legislative battle on behalf of the president. To say it was an uphill battle would be like calling Everest a mountain.

In the summer of 1981, President Reagan proposed to sell five Airborne Warning Control Systems (AWACS) jets to Saudi Arabia for $8.5 billion.[1] The jets had been leased to the Saudis since the Carter administration, and now the Saudis wanted to buy the planes.

Israeli Prime Minister Menachem Begin protested that the sale would violate Israel's "special relationship" with the United States.[2]

Under the Arms Export Control Act of 1974, the sale could be blocked if both Houses of Congress passed a joint resolution in opposition. Soon thereafter, all 100 members of the US Senate and all 435 members of the House of Representatives heard from the strong Israeli lobby. The House quickly voted against the sale, overwhelmingly rejecting the proposal by a vote of 301-111.[3]

The proposed sale also seemed doomed in the Senate, as fifty senators co-sponsored a resolution of disapproval.[4] With half the Senate supporting the resolution, only one more vote was needed to scuttle the sale.

But the White House was insistent that the new Senate majority leader should lead a come-from-behind victory.

Baker tried to give the White House a reality check, telling the president, "We've got twelve votes (in support of the sale), and that's counting me, and I don't want to vote for it."[5]

In the face of almost certain defeat, Baker began to build a bipartisan coalition. He reached out first to two Democrats: Sam Nunn of Georgia and David Boren of Oklahoma. Nunn was regarded on both sides of the aisle as *the* Senate expert on military affairs. Boren was head of the unofficial "conservative caucus" of Senate Democrats.

Senator Baker then reached out to a Republican, John Warner of Virginia, a former secretary of the Navy.

After conferring, Senators Nunn and Warner made a proposal to the majority leader. President Reagan should write a letter to the Senate, containing assurances that the Saudis had agreed to a "detailed plan" as to precisely how the AWACS jets would be used.

Senator Baker then turned to the president himself and asked him to engage in some old-fashioned retail politicking.[6] Some forty-four members of the Senate were invited to personal one-on-one meetings in the Oval Office with President Reagan. Many others would meet with the president in small groups. All totaled, Baker arranged for seventy-five members of the Senate to meet with the president and hear his personal appeal.

In the meetings in the Oval Office, the Great Communicator made his case to the senators.

"How can I convince foreign leaders I'm in command when I can't even sell five airplanes?"[7]

Baker then enlisted the support of three former occupants of the Oval Office. Richard Nixon, Gerald Ford, and Jimmy Carter sent

Senator Baker and Senate colleagues, 1981. Reprinted with the permission of Senator Baker and the Baker Center.

letters to the Senate endorsing the sale. Slowly and methodically, Baker began to turn the tide, persuading senators who had co-sponsored the resolution opposing the sale to reverse themselves and support the president.

But there was one member of the Senate who adamantly would not change his opposition to the AWACS sale. He was Republican Senator Robert Packwood of Oregon.

Baker had the greatest respect for his friend, Bob Packwood. While the two senators waged a vigorous legislative battle, they remained friends. As always, Baker treated his opponents with respect and dignity.

At 5 p.m. on October 28, 1981, with the outcome still in doubt, the Senate met for a roll-call vote on the proposed AWACS sale. As Baker awaited the vote, he looked up at the packed Senate gallery, and there he saw Georgie Packwood, wife of Senator Packwood. Mrs. Packwood was there to support her husband in his fight against the AWACS sale.[8]

Baker knew and liked Georgie Packwood. He was touched by the scene of her sitting there in support of her husband in a legislative battle with the president and the majority leader.

Since his days as a young trial lawyer in East Tennessee, Baker had always treated his opponents with civility. He would continue to do so throughout his public life, and particularly on this day of the culmination of a hard-fought political and legislative battle.

Baker motioned for an aide to come to him on the Senate floor. He told the aide that there were some roses in his office. And then he instructed the aide to get one of the roses and to take it into the gallery to Georgie Packwood.[9]

Baker would win his legislative battle that day with Robert Packwood. In perhaps the most dramatic come-from-behind victory in the history of the Senate, the AWACS sale went through by a vote of 52-48.

Packwood was bitterly disappointed. But in the years to come when he and Mrs. Packwood looked back on that historic day, what they would remember was not the vote. They would remember a civil moment. They would remember the moment that Baker delivered a rose to Mrs. Packwood.

CHAPTER 18

The Baker's Dozen

On October 12, 1984, Howard Baker and Robert Byrd met at the center aisle of the United States Senate and did what they had done at the beginning of each Senate session over the previous eight years. They shook hands. Baker would joke that he and the minority leader had "the janitor's job. Robert Byrd and I opened the Senate every morning."[1]

But that autumn day in 1984 would be the last time Baker and Byrd would extend that civil gesture. It would be Baker's last day on the Senate floor. Earlier in the year, the senator had announced that he was not going to seek a fourth term.[2] Baker viewed his life in eighteen-year cycles. For eighteen years, he had been a trial lawyer. For the next eighteen years he had been a US Senator. And now he was ready in the next era of his life to travel, write, and prepare for another White House run in 1988.

He also intended to make some money practicing law.

"When I came here (to the Senate)," Baker told the *Wall Street Journal*, "I was a wealthy, young lawyer . . . and I've gotten over all three."

On the final day of business of the 98th Senate session, the majority leader sat at his legislative desk as one by one his colleagues stood and bid him farewell.³

Baker was particularly moved by the tribute paid to him by Senator Mark Hatfield. The senior senator from Oregon was a deeply spiritual man, and he spoke of his admiration for the majority leader in spiritual terms:

> It is written, "A friend loves at all times, and a brother is born for adversity" (Proverbs 17:17).
>
> There are a great many relationships which are not born for adversity. Adversity is the wind which separates the chaff of flattery from the grain of solid, deep, and faithful friendship.
>
> Howard Baker has been the brother born for adversity for me and for many others. I am grateful for him, for his leadership, for his friendship, for his personal and political support, and for his patience with each of us as we have sought under his leadership to work for this venerable institution.
>
> A prophet of old said, "The best thing to give your enemy is forgiveness; to an opponent, tolerance; to a friend, your heart; to a child, your example; to a father, your deference; to your mother, conduct that makes her proud; to yourself, respect; and to all men, charity."
>
> Anyone who objectively reviews Howard Baker's public service record must conclude that on each count he has been faithful. Forgiveness, tolerance, and charitableness are part of his daily character; his capacity for heartfelt friendships, immense; his family life, truly exemplary; and his

Senator Baker, 1984. Reprinted with the permission of Senator Baker and the Baker Center.

> quiet confidence and strength, a sign of his peace with himself. I for one will miss him greatly and pray the best for him and his family in their new adventure.[4]

After many other tributes, the time came for the majority leader to bid farewell. In his final speech on the floor of the United States Senate, Howard Baker returned to his favorite topic, civility:

> The Senate cannot fight a guerrilla war over every issue all the time. We cannot be snipping at one another and talking issues to death while the essential work of government goes undone.

> That is not what the American people expect of us, and it is not what they will accept from us.
>
> If we cannot resurrect the spirit of chivalry that once reigned here, at least we may restore some semblance of civility and commonality of purpose in this time of challenges at home and abroad.[5]

Fifteen years later, on July 14, 1998, civilian Howard Baker would return to the Capitol at the invitation of majority leader Trent Lott to give a speech in the Leader's Lecture Series.

Baker entitled his remarks "On Herding Cats," and in this speech he again returned to the themes of civility and bipartisanship.

"What really makes the Senate work—as our heroes knew profoundly—is an understanding of human nature, an appreciation of the hearts, as well as the minds, the frailties as well as the strengths, of one's colleagues and constituents," he said.[6]

Baker shared some cherished memories of legislative battles fought during his years in the Senate:

> Very often in the course of my eighteen years in the Senate, and especially in the last eight years as Republican leader and then majority leader, I found myself engaged in fire-breathing, passionate debate with my fellow senators over the great issues of the times: Civil Rights, Vietnam, environmental protection, Watergate, the Panama Canal, tax cuts, defense spending, the Middle East, relations with the Soviet Union, and dozens more.
>
> But no sooner had the final word been spoken and the last vote taken than I would usually walk to the desk of my most recent antagonist, extend a hand of friendship, and solicit his support on the next issue for the following day.

> People must think we're crazy when we do that.
> Or perhaps they think our debates are fraudulent to begin with, if we could put our passion aside so quickly and embrace our adversaries so readily.
> But we aren't crazy and we aren't frauds.
> This ritual is as natural as breathing hard in the Senate, and it is as important as anything that happens in Washington or in the country we serve.[7]

And then, Howard Baker, the old East Tennessee Lincoln Republican, quoted from his favorite president: "We are not enemies but friends. We must not be enemies."[8] Baker added that civility "pulls us back from the brink of rhetorical, intellectual, even physical violence, that thank God, has only rarely disturbed the peace of the Senate. It makes us America, not Bosnia. It's what makes us the most stable government on Earth, not a civil war waiting to happen."

Baker concluded, "We are doing the business of the American people. We have to do it every day. And if we cannot be civil with one another—if we stop dealing with those who disagree with us or those we do not like, we would soon stop functioning altogether."

The former majority leader concluded his lecture by sharing "a few rules of Senate leadership." Thirteen of them, to be exact . . . an even Baker's Dozen.[9]

Baker's Rules of Senate Leadership

1. Understand its limits. The Senate leader relies on two prerogatives, neither of which is constitutionally or statutorily guaranteed. They are the right of prior recognition under the precedent of the Senate and the conceded right to schedule the Senate's business.

These together with the reliability of his commitment and whatever power of political persuasion one brings to the job, are all the tools a Senate leader has.

2. Have a genuine and decent respect for differing points of view. Remember that every senator is an individual with individual needs, ambitions, and political conditions. None was sent there to march in lockstep with his or her colleagues and none will. But also remember that even members of the opposition party are susceptible to persuasion and redemption on a surprising number of issues. Understanding these shifting sands is the beginning of wisdom for a Senate leader.

3. Consult as often as possible, with as many senators as possible, on as many issues as possible. This consultation should encompass not only committee chairmen but as many members of one's party conference as possible in matters of legislative scheduling.

4. Remember that senators are people with families. Schedule the Senate as humanely as possible, with as few all-night sessions and as much accommodation as you can manage.

5. Choose a good staff. In the complexity of today's world, it is impossible for a member to gather and digest all the information that is necessary for the member to make an informed and prudent decision on all the major issues. Listen to your staff, but don't let them fall into the habit of forgetting who works for whom.

6. Listen more than you speak. As my father-in-law, Everett Dirksen, once admonished me in my first year in this body, "Occasionally allow yourself the luxury of an unexpressed thought."

7. Count carefully, and often. The essential training of a Senate majority leader perhaps ends in the third grade, when he learns to count reliably. But fifty-one today may be forty-nine tomorrow, so keep on counting.

8. Work with the president, whoever he is, whenever possible. When I became leader after the elections of 1980, I had to decide whether I would try to set a separate agenda for the Senate or try to see how our new president, with a Republican Senate, could work together as a team to enact his programs. I chose the latter course, and history proved me right.

Would I have done the same with a president of the opposing party? Lyndon Johnson did with President Eisenhower, and history proved him right as well.

9. Work with the House. It is a co-equal branch of government, and nothing the Senate does, except in the ratification of treaties and the confirmation of federal officers, is final unless the House concurs. My father and stepmother both served in the House, and I appreciate its special role as the sounding board of American politics. John Rhodes and I established a Joint Leadership Office in 1977, and it worked very well. I commend that arrangement to this generation of Senate leaders and to every succeeding generation.

10. No surprises. Bob Byrd and I decided more than twenty years ago that while we were bound to disagree on many things, one thing we would always agree on was the need to keep each other fully informed. It was an agreement we never broke—not once—in the eight years we served together as Republican and Democrat leaders of the Senate.

11. Tell the truth, whether you have to or not. Remember that your word is the only currency you have to do business in the Senate. Devalue it, and your effectiveness as a Senate leader is over. And always get the bad news out first.

12. Be patient. The Senate was conceived by America's founders as "the saucer into which the nation's passions are poured to cool." Let senators have their say.

Bide your time—I worked for eighteen years to get television in the Senate and the first camera was not turned on until after I left. But patience and persistence have their shining reward. It is better to let a few important things be your legacy than to boast of a thousand bills that have no lasting significance.

13. Be civil, and encourage others to do likewise. Many of you have heard me speak of the need for greater civility in our political discourse. I have been making that speech since the late 1960s, when America turned into an armed battleground over the issues of civil rights and Vietnam.

Having seen political passion erupt into physical violence, I do not share the view of those who say that politics today are meaner or more debased than ever. But in this season of prosperity and peace, so rare in our national experience, it ill behooves America's leaders to invent disputes for the sake of political advantage, or to inveigh carelessly against motives and morals of one's political adversaries. America expects better of its leaders than this, and deserves better.

CHAPTER 19

Saving the President

Howard Baker was at the Miami Zoo doing two of his favorite things, entertaining his grandchildren and taking pictures.

Joy Baker was just a few miles away at the Baker vacation home in Bar Harbor. The phone rang in the Baker condo. When Joy answered it, the voice at the other end of the line asked her to hold for the president of the United States. Shortly thereafter, President Ronald Reagan came on the line and asked Joy if he could speak with "his old friend, Howard."

"He's at the zoo with the grandkids," Joy said.

"Well," President Reagan said, "wait until he sees the zoo I have in store for him!"[1]

Despite the typical Reagan humor, the president of the United States was in serious trouble. And he needed Howard Baker.

In February 1987, the White House was in disarray, and the president was on the defensive.[2]

On February 26, 1987, the Tower Commission had delivered to the president its report on the "Iran-Contra Affair," the complicated scenario that consisted of two concurrent initiatives that had secretly been undertaken by a number of the president's top aides in 1985 and 1986.³

First, senior Reagan administration officials had covertly facilitated the sale of arms to Iran. The goal was to secure an opening to "moderate elements" in the radical Iranian regime of the Ayatollah Ruhollah Khomeini as well as to secure the release of American hostages held in Beirut.

Second, funds from the arms sale had been diverted to military re-supply efforts to the rebels collectively known as the Contras, who were battling the Sandinista regime in Nicaragua.

Both covert initiatives clearly violated the law. Congress had passed an arms embargo against Iran, one of the world's leading sources of state-supported terrorism.

In 1982, Congress had passed the Boland Amendment that outlawed any US assistance to the Contras for the purpose of overthrowing the Nicaraguan government.

In April 1986, nationally syndicated columnists Jack Anderson and Dale Van Atta first broke the story of the secret initiatives.

Van Atta had first learned of the arms-for-hostages deal in December of 1985, but he had been asked by administration officials to hold the story, claiming that hostages might be killed if the initiative was publicized. President Reagan himself had had a one-on-one meeting with Van Atta on February 24, 1986, in which he urged Van Atta and Anderson to suppress the story. But by the fall of 1986, the story was not only out, it had become a full-blown scandal.⁴

On November 25, Attorney General Edwin Meese announced the discovery of the so-called "Diversion Memo" that had been authored by Lt. Col. Oliver North, a top aide to the president's National Security Council. North had ordered Major General Richard Secord, a retired Air Force officer, to make $2.6 million in profits from the Iran arms sale available to the Contras in Nicaragua.

President Ronald Reagan and White House Chief of Staff Howard Baker. Reprinted with the permission of Senator Baker and the Baker Center.

Meese announced that in light of the discovery of the Diversion Memo, a criminal investigation of the principals was beginning.

In a nationally televised speech, President Reagan insisted that the shipment to Iran involved "only small amounts of defensive weapons and spare parts." And he emphasized, "We did not—repeat—we did not trade weapons or anything else for hostages."[5]

On November 26, 1986, President Reagan had appointed the Tower Commission to investigate the Iran-Contra Affair. The commission consisted of former Senator John Tower, former Secretary of State Edmund Muskie, and former National Security Adviser Brent Scowcroft.

On February 26, 1987, the commission had issued its report, and it was scathing.[6] Contrary to the statements made by President Reagan, the commission found that "an arms-for-hostages" trade had taken place in violation of the US arms embargo against Iran, and that it "rewarded a regime that clearly supported terrorism." The report further found that the aide to the Contras was in conflict with congressional action that had barred either direct or indirect support of military operations in Nicaragua.

While the Tower Commission report had not directly implicated the president, the report's assessment of his leadership was devastating. The report portrayed the president as confused and detached. While the report quoted the president as saying he had no knowledge of the diversion of Iranian arms profits to the Contras, the report bluntly stated that his leadership style had allowed aides to run amok in implementing secret policies in violation of the law.

Congress was launching an investigation, and increasingly, the word "impeachment" was being heard.

To make matters worse, Chief of Staff Donald Regan had lost the confidence of the president. Even more significantly, he'd lost the confidence of First Lady Nancy Reagan.[7]

Donald Regan's leadership style as chief of staff was consistent with his style as a blunt, tough Wall Street executive. He ran the 325-person White House staff with efficiency, but he was arrogant and condescending, boasting that he, rather than the president, had decision-making power in the White House. Worse, he frequently made comments that were critical of his boss, the president.[8]

For months leading up to February 1987, Nancy Reagan and close friends of the president had become increasingly upset about Donald Regan's leadership style and his comments as chief of staff. Ed Rollins, who had served as President Reagan's 1984 campaign manager, was blunt in his assessment:

> Don Regan was a tyrant. And he was miscast as a chief of staff and never thought of himself as staff. He thought of himself as deputy president. (He) said to me one day, "I can make eighty-five percent of the decisions the president makes."
>
> And I said to him, I said, "Don, I just ran a campaign in fifty states. I didn't see your name on the ballot anywhere."[9]

Mrs. Reagan had made her feelings known to Michael Deaver, the Washington lobbyist, Stewart Spencer, the president's political consultant, George Will, the nationally syndicated columnist, and Nancy Reynolds, a close friend.

Mrs. Reagan became enraged when she read a quote from Donald Regan in the *New York Times* in November 1986 that he was "running the shovel brigade to clean up after the president." [10]

In January 1987, the president had prostate surgery. The First Lady believed that the chief of staff had pushed her husband to deliver the State of the Union message on January 27, just three weeks after the surgery.

Nancy Reagan was not the only member of the president's family who intensely disliked the chief of staff. Maureen Reagan, the president's daughter, had had several run-ins with the chief of staff, including at least one "shouting match over the telephone." [11]

During another phone conversation with the first lady, the chief of staff had abruptly hung up on her during the course of a heated argument.

The first lady returned the favor during a phone conversation with the chief of staff just days before the anticipated release of the Tower Commission report. Donald Regan was insisting that the president hold a news conference shortly after the report's release. Mrs. Reagan strongly opposed this, and she communicated her opposition in no uncertain terms in a phone conversation. When Donald Regan would not back down, the first lady lost her temper and shouted, "Have your damn news conference!" She then slammed down the phone.

It was the last straw for Nancy Reagan. She told her husband that Donald Regan had to go, and the president reluctantly agreed.

On February 18, the president met with Donald Regan, and it was agreed that Mr. Regan would depart after the release of the Tower Commission report.

A search began for Regan's replacement.

While the president's top aides were involved, it was clearly the first lady who led the search.

The initial consensus was that the job should go to the president's old friend, Paul Laxalt, who had recently left the Senate and had returned to law practice.[12]

Richard Wirthlin, the White House pollster, was asked to make the call to Laxalt.

Paul Laxalt's response was that he was not the right person for the job, but he did have a suggestion.

He met with President Reagan in the president's study in the White House residence. Laxalt told his good friend that he wanted to exclude himself from serving in the White House.

"But I do have a name you should consider," he said.

The name Laxalt gave the president was the name of the man Laxalt had nominated for majority leader of the United States Senate in 1981, Howard Baker.[13]

The first lady enthusiastically endorsed the idea. The president's senior advisers agreed. As one later explained, "Howard Baker had everything that we needed. We had to rebuild our bridges to Congress, especially leveraging our Republican coalition in the Senate. We had to have somebody who was immediately recognized as a strong and confident individual, not only by the press but by the Washington establishment. We needed someone who knew the legislative process. We needed someone with a sense of the political nuances going into a presidential election campaign. We needed someone with whom the president could be comfortable. We needed someone who already had established that bond of trust and immediate support in Washington."[14]

So the call went to Howard Baker. When he returned from the zoo and received the president's offer, he immediately accepted. He agreed, on the condition that he could bring with him to the White House two of his closest advisers, A.B. Culvahouse and Tom Griscom.

Culvahouse had joined then-Senator Baker's staff as a legislative assistant in 1973 after graduating from NYU Law School. Culvahouse's first assignment was to sit directly behind Senator Baker in the Watergate hearings so the senator and his new young assistant "could get to know one another."[15] It was the beginning of a strong working relationship that would last for decades.

Since Baker's departure from the Senate in 1985, he and Culvahouse had practiced law together at Vinson and Elkins, where Culvahouse was quickly rising as a Washington super lawyer. With Baker's arrival as chief of staff, Culvahouse would be the new White House legal counsel.

Tom Griscom was Baker's former press secretary, and the man who had been standing by Baker in Iowa in January 1980, when the senator refused to attack President Jimmy Carter on the grain embargo. Griscom would be named the new White House communications director.[16]

Baker also brought with him to his White House transition team his longtime aide, James Cannon. Cannon had been a domestic policy adviser to President Gerald Ford and had served as Baker's chief of staff in Baker's years as Senate leader.

Over the weekend before their first day on the job, the new White House chief of staff assigned Griscom and Cannon to conduct an audit of the White House staff.[17] Griscom and Cannon interviewed every senior official at the White House. Cannon, in particular, was alarmed by what he learned. The staff was in chaos, and a number of Reagan staffers close to Donald Regan questioned whether the president was physically and mentally able to continue to function as commander in chief.

Cannon immediately communicated this to Baker and Culvahouse. They, along with Griscom, quickly convened at Baker's home. Cannon submitted a confidential memorandum to the new chief of staff that went so far as to raise the possibility of invoking the Twenty-Fifth Amendment to have Vice President

Bush take over as "acting president." In the memorandum, Cannon informed Baker that aides to Donald Regan had told him that the president "wasn't interested in the job. They said he wouldn't read the papers they gave him—even short position papers and documents. They said he wouldn't come over to work—all he wanted to do was watch movies and television at the residence."[18]

Baker listened to Cannon, but was skeptical. He had spent time the previous evening with the president.

"This doesn't sound like the Ronald Reagan I just saw, but we'll see tomorrow," Baker said.[19]

On the following day, Baker met in the Oval Office with President Reagan. He talked with him and listened to him. Baker "didn't see an AWOL president." The Ronald Reagan he saw was energetic, engaged, and in command.

Baker had also asked Culvahouse and Griscom to observe the president closely and see if they saw any evidence supporting Cannon's concerns.

Baker, Culvahouse, and Griscom had lunch with the president in the Cabinet Room. Afterward, the new chief of staff conferred privately with Culvahouse and Griscom and gave his assessment.

"Boys, this is a fully functional and capable president," he declared.[20]

Culvahouse and Griscom agreed.

Baker then dismissed Cannon's concern about the president's competency, telling senior staff members, "I don't want to hear any more talk about that."

The new chief of staff then turned his attention to helping the president prepare for a nationally televised speech.

Fourteen years earlier, Baker had counseled a president who faced a scandal to be open and candid with Congress and the American people. President Nixon did not listen to Howard Baker, but Ronald Reagan did. In his March 4 speech from the Oval Office, President Reagan confessed, "I told the American people that I did not trade arms for hostages. My heart and my best intentions still tell me that is true. But the facts and the evidence tell me it is not. . . . What began as a strategic opening to Iran deteriorated in its implementation into trading arms for hostages."[21]

Following this speech, Baker then began to do what he had done in his eighteen years in the United States Senate. He reached out to his friends in Congress, to seek their support on behalf of President Reagan.[22]

He returned to his old office, S-231, now occupied by the Senate minority leader, Bob Dole. But S-231 had a new name. The suite was now called "The Howard H. Baker Jr. Room," and featured a portrait of the former majority leader.

As the new chief of staff walked into his old office, he said, "It's like coming home. I'm just visiting a few old friends."

Senator Dole said he would like to give Baker a key so that he could visit whenever he liked.

"Don't bother," replied Baker. "I kept my key."[23]

The new chief of staff then spent the day visiting many of his former congressional colleagues as well as meeting ones that had arrived in Congress since his departure.

Baker visited with his old friend Bob Byrd, and also with House Speaker Jim Wright and Republican House leader Robert Michael.

Both Democrats and Republicans in Congress greeted Howard Baker with open arms. *New York Times* syndicated columnist Maureen Dowd quoted Senator Charles Schumer of New York saying, "For the Democrats during the Donald Regan era, all we got was thunderbolts coming down from the White House. We never really talked about things."

And Republican Senator Alan Simpson was quoted as saying, "Donald Regan was always of the opinion that it was our duty on Capitol Hill to make tough decisions. He would want support on some program, and we'd say, 'It's politically impossible' and he'd say, 'You guys are paid to do the politically impossible.'"²⁴

"He (Regan) did not have the political sense to understand how to be pragmatic," Simpson said. "Baker has it running out of his toes."²⁵

Baker then reached out to an old friend and fellow Tennessean. He was the man he had first met on a spring day in 1964 at the offices of the *Tennessean* newspaper. John Seigenthaler had returned to Washington in 1987 as editorial director for *USA Today*.

Baker called not only Seigenthaler, but also John Chancellor of *NBC News* and columnist George Will. The new chief of staff requested an "off-the-record" meeting with these three influential journalists.²⁶

All three agreed to the meeting. Seigenthaler recalled that at the meeting, Baker conducted himself remarkably like he had at their first meeting at the offices of the *Tennessean* in 1964. He thanked the three for meeting with him and freely acknowledged the task he had as the president's chief of staff.

"Howard was Reagan's lawyer that day; he was his advocate," Seigenthaler recalled. "He was making a case (to us) that this country is going to be better off if you help me get this president over the fence that he has gotten upon."

It was classic Howard Baker strategic civility. He freely acknowledged to these three powerful journalists that he knew he had a tough task ahead, and he hoped he would have their support.

But while the new chief of staff was reaching out to friends and powerful interests outside the White House, he was also conducting an intense internal investigation at 1600 Pennsylvania Avenue.²⁷ To defend the president in the upcoming congressional Iran-Contra investigation, Baker had to address the same compound question he had posed in the Watergate hearings in 1973: What did the president know, and when did the president know it?

Baker asked the new White House Counsel A.B. Culvahouse to find the answer to the question. Impressing upon Culvahouse the gravity of the situation, Baker flatly told him, "You do not want to be the first counsel to the president to have his client tried and convicted in an impeachment trial."[28]

Culvahouse spent weeks investigating documents and interviewing witnesses, including the president on numerous occasions. He sought to determine what Ronald Reagan knew and when he knew it.

After painstakingly reviewing White House logs, reading the president's diary, and interviewing scores of witnesses who had met with the president on national security matters, Culvahouse found no evidence indicating that Ronald Reagan knew of the diversion of funds before Attorney General Meese had discovered the "diversion memorandum" on November 25, 1986. Culvahouse also concluded that there was no legal theory that would sustain an impeachment conviction.[29]

Baker and Culvahouse then did exactly what Baker had advised President Nixon to do in 1973. They contacted Iran-Contra committee chairman Daniel Inouye and Vice Chairman Warren Rudman as well as House Counterparts Lee Hamilton and Richard Cheney and shared with them the documents they believed established that while President Reagan had not exercised effective management and control over his national security staff, he had not been aware of illegal activities or sought to cover them up.[30]

Over the next few months as the congressional investigation continued, the chief of staff continued to reach out to his former colleagues with candor and transparency.

On May 5 through August 3, 1987, the US Senate Select Committee on Secret Military Assistance to Iran and the Nicaraguan Opposition, as well as the US House Select Committee to Investigate Covert Arms Transactions with Iran, met jointly. Over the course of forty days of public hearings, twenty-eight witnesses testified, and over a thousand administration documents were entered into the record.[31]

At the urging of his chief of staff and his White House counsel, the president, in contrast to Richard Nixon, waived executive privilege not only for his aides and their documents, but also for himself. He even provided the committee with access to his personal diary.

On July 15, 1987, President Reagan's former national security adviser, Admiral John Poindexter, testified before the Joint Committee. In his testimony, he answered Howard Baker's old question on what the president knew and when did he know it. "I made a very deliberate decision not to ask the president, so that I could insulate him from the decision and provide some future deniability for the president if it ever leaked out," the admiral bluntly testified. "The buck stops here, with me."[32]

> "I let my preoccupation with the hostages intrude in the areas where it didn't belong."
> —President Reagan

While Poindexter's testimony was criticized by many as incredible, it was clear that there was no smoking gun connecting President Reagan to knowledge of the covert initiatives or a cover-up of them.

When the hearings concluded on August 12, President Reagan gave another nationally televised address, at the urging of his chief of staff. He candidly told the American people, "Our original initiative rapidly got all tangled up in the sale of arms, and the sale of arms got tangled up with the hostages. I let my preoccupation with the hostages intrude in the areas where it didn't belong . . . I was stubborn in my pursuit of a policy that went astray."[33]

On November 18, 1987, the congressional committee released the report of their findings. It was not flattering. The report clearly stated that "the Iran-Contra affair was characterized by pervasive dishonesty and inordinate secrecy."[34] The report further found that the actions of many senior White House officials amounted to a blatant circumvention of the arms embargo on Iran and the

Boland Amendment, and that the law was violated and Congress deceived. The report's findings about the president were stinging:

> ... The ultimate responsibility for the events in the Iran-Contra affair must rest with the president. If the president did not know what his national security advisers were doing, he should have. It is his responsibility to communicate unambiguously to his subordinates that they must keep him advised of important actions they take for the administration. The Constitution requires the president to "take care that the laws be faithfully executed." This charge encompasses a responsibility to leave the members of his administration in no doubt that the rule of law governs.[35]

But the report made no findings that the president himself actually knew of illegal activities or worked to conceal them.

Fourteen Reagan administration officials would be indicted, including Secretary of Defense Casper Weinberger. But there would be no impeachment, and Ronald Wilson Reagan would be allowed to serve the last fourteen months of his presidency.

Baker would continue to serve as President Reagan's chief of staff for seven months, leading the White House staff with characteristic Baker civility. In contrast to Donald Regan, Baker did not see himself as a "deputy president" or "prime minister." One observer described his style as follows:

> Baker, as an established political figure in his own right, stands out from the crowd as the most senior presidential confidant and counselor. But his prime mission is to assure that a range of advisory voices is heard in the Oval Office.

> Unlike his predecessor, Donald T. Regan, who sought to formalize the West Wing chain of reporting relationships, Baker is using a staffing strategy that counts upon cooperation among team players of supposedly co-equal standing. As befits a creature of the legislative branch, his style of operation tends toward the collegial rather than the hierarchical.[36]

As White House chief of staff, Baker also reached out to Democrats, just as he had done during his years as Republican Senate leader.

One day in 1987, Baker learned that Senator Al Gore was announcing his candidacy for the 1988 Democratic presidential nomination. Gore had been elected to Baker's Senate seat in 1984 after Baker had decided not to seek a fourth term.[37]

When the White House chief of staff heard about Senator Gore's announcement, he tried to reach him to congratulate him. Baker explained to the *New York Times*'s Steven Roberts, "I was thinking that I should mark this day somehow. I served in the Senate with Al's father and I have known this young man since he was a boy. I thought about calling Al directly, but then realized I couldn't do that on a White House phone. I thought about calling his father, but Al Senior talked too much. So I called his mother, Pauline. 'Howard,' she said immediately, 'I know why you are calling me. I am the only Gore in town you can count on to keep her mouth shut.'"[38]

Ever the loyal Republican, Baker could still reach out to his Democratic colleagues and friends and wish them the best.

Baker stepped down on July 1, 1988, to spend time caring for both his wife, Joy, and his stepmother, Irene, both of whom had been experiencing health problems.

Baker's tenure as chief of staff had both its successes and its setbacks. By the fall of 1987, many of Baker's former colleagues on Capitol Hill were blaming the chief of staff for a number of problems in the Reagan administration, including such notable legislative defeats as the rejection of the nominations of Judge Robert Bork and Judge Douglas Ginsburg for the Supreme Court, and the overriding of a Reagan veto of a mass transit bill.[39]

Baker was highly criticized for his conciliatory style. Former White House communications director Pat Buchanan wrote of the chief of staff, ". . . a decent honorable man of the middle, Howard Baker does not understand the us-versus-them politics of the flank that today dominates both parties."

Senator William Cohen came to the defense of his old Senate colleague.

"The focus from the president's fall from grace has now shifted to the very man who rescued him from disaster," Cohen said.

Senator Cohen's conclusion was shared by John Seigenthaler. In Seigenthaler's opinion, there was no doubt that the strategic civility of Howard Baker had saved the presidency of Ronald Reagan.[40]

President Ronald Reagan and White House Chief of Staff Howard Baker meet in the Oval Office. Reprinted with the permission of Senator Baker and the Baker Center.

"Senator, you just made some of the strangest new friends and some of the maddest old ones!"

—*Lonnie Strunk, longtime friend of Howard Baker Jr., after a controversial vote*

CHAPTER 20

A Gentle Tennessee Wit

There are many qualities that President Reagan admired in his chief of staff, Howard Baker. But at the top of the list is what the president referred to as Baker's "gentle Tennessee wit."[1]

Reagan and Baker shared an affinity for stories. They liked to tell stories. They liked to hear stories.

Both were master storytellers. Reagan had perfected the art not only during his years as an actor, but during his decades on the speaking circuit.

Baker had developed his talent of storytelling during his years as a trial lawyer, and had perfected it on the campaign trails in Tennessee and in the halls of Congress.

For decades, both men had used stories to inspire and persuade audiences and to defuse tense situations.

Baker was fond of saying of his friend Senator Bob Dole, "He can put things in perspective with wit and humor more effectively than most philosophers can do with a serious dissertation, and I admire that."

While Bob Dole appreciated the compliment, he responded that no one in public life used humor better than Howard Baker.

"I just do quips, one-liners," said Dole. "Howard tells great stories."

And so when Baker became President Reagan's chief of staff, these two great storytellers started a daily ritual. They would begin each working day in the Oval Office by meeting and sharing with one another a favorite story.[2]

There is no record of the stories they shared. The Nixon taping system in the Oval Office had long been dismantled. But the president no doubt heard many of the stories that Baker had shared over the years with colleagues, friends, and voters.

> *"I just do quips, one-liners. Howard tells great stories."*
> —Senator Bob Dole

One of Baker's favorite stories dated back to his days as a young trial lawyer. After the first day of a long and difficult trial, Baker and his client returned to the law offices of Baker and Baker, where they were greeted by Howard Baker Sr.

"How is the trial going?" the elder Baker asked his son.

Baker Jr. knew it was not going well, but he didn't want to say so in front of his client. Deflecting the question, he looked at his client and said, "Well, how do *you* think it's going?"

"They are telling lies about me!" thundered the client. "And worse yet," he added, "they are proving most of them!"[3]

During his years in the Senate, Baker would enjoy regaling his colleagues with stories poking gentle fun at the very institution they served, the United States Senate.

He liked to tell the story of the old couple that was touring the Capitol, when suddenly they were astounded by the sound of clanging bells and strident buzzers. They had no idea these were the traditional signals sounded in the Capitol to alert senators that a floor vote was imminent.

"What's that?" the woman asked.

"I don't know," her husband replied, "but one of them may have escaped!"

Another story Baker loved was about the time someone asked Will Rogers, "Is it true that Congress is made up entirely of thieves and rascals?" The senator would recount Will Roger's reply: "Of course it's true, but it's a good cross-section of its constituency."

Baker's favorite stories were invariably ones where he was the foil of the joke. He particularly liked to share stories on how his close friend and pilot, Lonnie Strunk, had kept Baker's ego in check during his time as a Senate leader.

On one occasion after Senator Baker had cast a vote on an issue that was very controversial back in Tennessee, Lonnie told him, "Senator, you just made some of the strangest new friends and some of the maddest old ones!"[4]

In January of 1981, after his election as majority leader, Baker was honored at a black-tie dinner in Washington. The guest list was a who's who of Washington power brokers. But Baker also made sure that his old friend Lonnie Strunk was in attendance and also arranged for him to be a speaker.

One dignitary after another spoke at the dinner, all heaping praise upon the new majority leader.

And then it was Lonnie Strunk's turn at the podium.

Baker loved to quote Lonnie's toast that night:

> When we were boys growing up in Tennessee, I used to work for Howard Baker's family.
>
> I'd be out there on Saturday afternoons washing the car or cutting their lawn, and I used to think about what would happen to us when we grew up.
>
> I always knew I'd end up wearing a tuxedo and speaking at a dinner like this . . . but I'd never thought he'd be here.[5]

Baker absolutely loved telling that story.

President Reagan loved hearing it.

It was indeed gentle Tennessee wit, and it was at the heart of the civility of Howard Baker.

CHAPTER 21

The View from Both Ends of Pennsylvania Avenue

Having served eighteen years in the Senate and eighteen months as White House Chief of Staff, Howard Baker had a unique perspective on Pennsylvania Avenue. He had worked on both ends of "that famous stretch of road," and he felt it was very important that it become a two-way street.

On March 16, 1990, Baker gave the keynote address for the 21st annual Student Symposium of the Center for the Study of the Presidency. He entitled his remarks, "The View from Both Ends of the Avenue."[1]

The speech was a clarion call for civility and bipartisanship in public life.

Baker began his speech by recalling the friendship of his late father-in-law, Everett Dirksen, with President Lyndon Johnson. "It was a bond of fundamental trust and personal good will between those men," Baker remembered, "and it was well understood that if a national crisis should suddenly arise, the president of the United

States and the Republican leader of the Senate could counsel frankly and deal effectively with one another."

Sadly, Baker noted "that kind of relationship simply doesn't exist much in Washington anymore."

Then in words that would be prophetic, Baker noted that the breakdown of communication and civility in Washington had put "a serious strain on the ability of the executive and legislative branches to do anything important together . . . (particularly) in efforts to reduce the federal budget deficit."

Five years after this speech, the federal government would in fact shut down for several days due to a stalemate between the White House and Congress. Twenty years later, the federal government would be perched on a "fiscal cliff" due to the inability of Congress and the White House to reach an agreement on reducing the federal deficit.

Critically examining the institution he loved and had led for years, Baker stated, "I believe the modern Congressman spends far too much time engaging in bureaucratic warfare with the executive branch and far too little time functioning as the national board of directors as the Constitution intended it to be."

The speech then focused on two ideas that Baker had been promoting for years. The first was a return to the concept of citizen legislators:

> It hasn't been so long ago that members of Congress were real people with real jobs and real communities throughout the country. They were truly representative of the people who elected them—and had the moral and political authority of true representatives—because they played an active, integral part in the civil and economic and social affairs of their constituencies. They went to Washington temporarily, and they came home.

Senator Howard Baker on "Face The Nation." Reprinted with the permission of *CBS News*.

Baker recalled for years how when his father served in Congress in the 1950s, he would get on a train to Washington every January and come home on a return ticket by the end of May.

"By the time I got to the Senate in 1967, two things had changed," recalled Baker. "First, there were planes instead of trains, and second, the job lasted all year long."

Baker did not feel either change was a real advancement.

Baker urged in his speech that Congress could do better "not by doing more, but by doing less."

He said, "I believe that Congress could do everything it really needs to do in about six months; a few months early in the year to decide what to spend money on, and the few months near the end of the year to decide how much to spend."

Baker then added, "I would propose that the rest of the year be spent not in Washington, but in America, seeing first-hand the practical effects of federal laws on private lives and enterprise, staying in personal touch with the people they're elected to represent, experiencing life as the rest of us know it—and drawing the authority from such close encounters with real people to tell a president he is full of beans when he proposes something out of kilter with the real world."

The second idea Baker advanced was one he had advocated during his brief campaign for the White House in 1980, a small branch office for the president.

> The president, for his part, could do with a little less remoteness from the Congress itself. The president used to have a working office in the Capitol building, and I think we should open that office again.
>
> The symbolism of a president and the Congress physically working together is as obvious as it is important. But the practical implications are a great deal more important.

Sadly, Baker noted, the president now "comes to Capitol Hill only a few times a year . . . for a speech, and Congress responds with a cacophony of criticism for nearly everything the president has to say."

Baker noted that a "greater proximity" between the president and Congress "would do wonders for our politics" if for no other reason than because "it's harder to say nasty things about somebody you have to see in the hallway every day."

Baker concluded the speech by calling for a fundamental change in the prevailing political atmosphere in Washington:

> I believe we have to start thinking about things a little differently in this country. While holding fast to our principles, we must have a decent respect for differing points of view.
>
> We must understand that after the time of testing comes the time for uniting. We must recognize that it is the resolution of conflict—rather than the perpetuation of conflict—that makes the difference between successful self-government and civil warfare.

Baker freely acknowledged that what he said in his speech that day were things he had been "saying . . . for about twenty years now, on both ends of Pennsylvania Avenue," and that he was under no illusion "that anyone would pay any more attention now than when I stood at the center of power."

Baker then concluded his speech expressing the hope that "civility in our politics is an idea whose time has come at last, and none too soon."

Howard and Joy Baker on their wedding day, 1951. Reprinted with the permission of Senator Baker and the Baker Center.

CHAPTER 22

The Cherry Blossom Romance

Joy Dirksen Baker passed away on April 24, 1993, after a multi-year battle with many health issues including cancer.[1]

Howard and Joy Baker had met at the 1951 Cherry Blossom Ball in Washington.

Howard was attending because his sister Mary was the 1951 Tennessee Cherry Blossom Princess. Joy Dirksen was there in her capacity as Illinois Cherry Blossom Princess.

It was not exactly love at first sight. On their first encounter, Howard Baker found the two princesses smoking. Young Howard accused the Illinois Cherry Blossom Princess of being a "very corruptive influence" on the Tennessee Cherry Blossom Princess. He promptly took his sister into his custody and shoved Joy Dirksen into a rose bush. It was an anomalous uncivil act in Baker's otherwise civil life.[2]

A few days later, an embarrassed Howard Baker decided an apology was definitely in order. He called the Dirksen family home in Washington, asked to speak to the Illinois Cherry Blossom Princess, and requested a personal meeting with her Royal Highness.

The apology turned out to be incredibly effective. Howard and Joy were married just a few months later.

The Cherry Blossom romance lasted for forty-two years. Contrary to appearance, it was not a political marriage.

While Joy Dirksen was the daughter of a United States senator and had faithfully worked in her father's campaigns, she did not like politics. She resented how it had caused long periods of separation from her father.

When Howard Baker announced for the Senate in 1964, Joy Baker complained, only half-jokingly, that she thought she had married a "country lawyer, and he turned out to be a politician."[3]

Joy Baker campaigned for her husband, just as she had for her father, but she did so quietly, seldom making a speech.

In the summer of 1976, politics had caused considerable pain to Joy Dirksen Baker, and consequently, to her husband as well.[4]

After the death of her father in 1969, Joy struggled with depression that led to a long bout with alcoholism. It had been a terrible battle, but by 1975, Joy had quit drinking.

At the 1976 Republican National Convention, Howard had made the short list for President Gerald Ford's vice presidential pick. The vetting process required Senator Baker to answer questions about not only his personal health history, but his family's as well. With Joy's blessing, Howard fully disclosed to the Ford team that Joy was a recovering alcoholic.

On the opening night of the GOP Convention in Kansas City, Howard and Joy Baker walked hand-in-hand to the convention podium to the sounds of the "Tennessee Waltz." He then gave the keynote address of the convention, and to use a Tennessee phrase, it was a barn-burner. Baker talked honestly about Watergate and how it had been painful for him and for his party. The Republicans, he said, "faced our problems with honor and dignity." He then hit on basic conservative themes, saying the primary issues of the 1976 campaign would be, "How much government is too much government? How many laws are too many laws? How much taxation is too much taxation? How much coercion is too much coercion?"[5]

On the issue of the growing federal deficit, he quoted his father-in-law, Everett Dirksen: "Why, we spend a billion dollars here and a billion dollars there, and the first thing you know it adds up to real money."

The delegates loved it.

Howard Baker the trial lawyer was making the opening statement for the Republican Presidential Campaign, and the jury he was addressing was not the delegates in the convention hall, but millions of Americans watching on television.[6] He was using the medium of television just as he had done on the campaign trail in Tennessee in 1966 to beat Frank Clement, and just as he had done in the Watergate hearings in 1973.

At the conclusion of the speech, the delegates erupted with cries of "Ford-Baker!"[7] Convention chairman Bob Dole called Howard Baker back to the podium for two curtain calls and, with characteristic Dole deadpan humor said, "This guy may have a future in politics."

Suddenly Howard Baker was the odds-on favorite to be nominated for vice president. John Seigenthaler observed that the only unanswered question going into the 1976 presidential election was whether "Ford had the good sense to pick Baker."

But on the morning after the speech, Baker's press secretary, Ron McMahon, got a phone call from a reporter. The information on the Baker family health history that had been disclosed to the Ford campaign team was supposed to be confidential, but someone had leaked it. The reporter asked McMahon to comment on the report that Joy was a recovering alcoholic. McMahon asked Baker what to do, and without hesitation, Baker responded, "Confirm it."[8]

And then the story took a nasty turn. Joy had been in a fender-bender car accident in Washington a week before the convention.

Nationally syndicated columnist Jack Anderson wrote a story about it, implying that Joy had been drunk at the time of the accident.[9]

A.B. Culvahouse quickly flew back to Washington and gathered the police reports that clearly established that the accident was simply a fender bender, nothing more and nothing less. The reports were immediately delivered to President Ford's vice presidential candidate vetting team along with confirmation that Joy had not had a drink in over a year.[10]

But the damage was done. President Ford chose Bob Dole as his running mate, and the Baker family made a quick exit back to Tennessee.

It was a painful episode for a woman who loved her husband dearly but would have been more than happy having remained the wife of a Tennessee trial lawyer.

Four years later, during her husband's brief campaign for the presidency, Joy was at her husband's side, campaigning in New Hampshire and Massachusetts and Maine, but she was a reluctant warrior who did not shed tears when the campaign ended.

Joy spent the last few years of her life fighting a number of afflictions including ulcers, bronchitis, chronic back pain, and ultimately cancer.

After leaving the Reagan White House in 1988, Howard renewed his law practice, but he then spent much of the next five years of his life taking care of Joy.

The Cherry Blossom romance lasted over four decades, until Joy passed away in Huntsville on an early spring evening in 1993.

CHAPTER 23

To Form a More Perfect Union

One evening in 1996, Howard Baker walked into the Capitol Grille in Washington to have dinner with his friends Marlene and Lawrence Eagleburger. Upon his arrival, he was met not only by the Eagleburgers, but by Nancy Landon Kassebaum, the junior senator from Kansas.[1]

It was a blind date that had been set up by Marlene Eagleburger.

Baker had first met Nancy Kassebaum in 1978, shortly after her election to the Senate.[2]

Her predecessor had resigned early to give her a chance to gain a little seniority, and so she was sworn in as a senator not in Washington, but in Topeka, Kansas.

Baker, the Republican leader of the Senate, flew to Topeka for the ceremony.

In their years together in the Senate, Nancy Kassebaum admired Baker for his sense of humor, his collegiality, and his kindness, even to his adversaries. She had witnessed the moment when Baker sent a rose to Mrs. Packwood, and she had been very impressed.

Nancy Kassebaum was the daughter of Alf Landon, the Kansas governor who was the Republican presidential nominee in 1936. Eleven-year-old Howard Baker had campaigned with his father for Governor Alf Landon in Tennessee that year.

In 1987, Baker had attended Alf Landon's 100th birthday party and had enjoyed swapping stories with the governor.[3]

The blind date in the Capitol Grille went well. To the delight of Marlene Eagleburger, Howard and Nancy had a very nice evening and clearly enjoyed each other's company.[4]

A few days later, he built up his courage, called the junior senator from Kansas, and asked her out on a non-blind date. She immediately accepted.

A nervous Howard Baker arrived at Senator Kassebaum's home in Northwest Washington wearing his best blue suit.[5] He rang the doorbell and then, as he would recall years later, "I stood on one foot and then the other until she came to the door."

"I feel like a sixteen-year-old," he said after greeting her.

"You don't look like sixteen," Nancy responded.

Baker escorted his date to his car and opened the passenger door for her like a true southern gentleman.

After securing Senator Kassebaum in the passenger's seat, Baker climbed into the driver's seat and released what he thought was the parking brake. But it wasn't the brake lever he had pulled.

The car's hood promptly popped open.

Nancy Kassebaum laughed hysterically, but on their second date, she insisted she do the driving.

On December 7, 1996, Nancy Landon Kassebaum and Howard H. Baker Jr. were married at St. Alban's Episcopal Church in Washington.[6]

The ceremony was performed by the Reverend John C. Danforth, an Episcopal priest who had served in the Senate with the senator bride and the senator groom.

A few days before the wedding, Father/Senator Danforth called

Senator Howard Baker and Senator Nancy Kassebaum Baker. Reprinted with the permission of Senator Baker and the Baker Center.

his old friend Howard to discuss the wedding plans. He explained that the tradition in the Episcopal church was for the minister to give a brief sermon or homily as part of a wedding ceremony.[7]

"Would you and Nancy like for me to do this at your wedding?" he asked.

Without hesitation, Baker responded, "No, Jack. Nancy and I have heard you speak enough over the years."

There was really no need for a homily. The invitation Cissy Baker personally wrote for the rehearsal dinner had said it all. It read, "In order to form a more perfect union, the distinguished gentleman from Tennessee yields the balance of his time to the distinguished gentlewoman from Kansas."[8]

Ambassador Howard Baker. Reprinted with the permission of Senator Baker and the Baker Center.

"There is a special, unique relationship that exists between the United States and Japan. It is remarkable, indeed, that given our history and relationship, that Japan and the United States would develop this strong bond, this mutuality of respect, this shared common view of the necessity for peace in the world."

—Howard Baker, in remarks after being sworn in as US ambassador to Japan

CHAPTER 24

Ambassador Baker: Civility on the World Stage

On June 26, 2001, 350 people gathered in the East Room of the White House for the swearing-in of the 38th ambassador to Japan. Typically, swearing-in ceremonies of ambassadors are private affairs conducted in a businesslike manner in the Oval Office. But the position of ambassador to Japan is no ordinary diplomatic post, and the man who was being sworn in as ambassador that day was no ordinary politician.

In the words of President George W. Bush, "We call upon one of America's most valued statesmen to help be the keeper of one of America's most valued friendships."[1]

President Bush had nominated Howard Baker for the position three months earlier on the recommendation of Secretary of State Colin Powell.[2] The president had approached Howard and Nancy Baker (as Senator Kassebaum now insisted she be called) at a dinner party hosted by Katherine Graham, publisher of the *Washington Post*. Taking Howard Baker aside, the president had directly appealed to him, "Howard, I'm serious. I really want you to be ambassador to Japan."

Baker had responded immediately.

"If that's what you really want, I will accept."

The president's announcement of his nomination was welcomed with unrestrained enthusiasm on Capitol Hill.

"Howard will be subjected to a vigorous confirmation process that will last about twelve seconds," Senator Joe Biden quipped.

When the president and the Bakers walked into the East Room for the swearing-in ceremony, they were greeted with a warm ovation by an audience that included Justice Sandra Day O'Connor, the vice president, the secretary of state, several former secretaries of state, cabinet officials, and congressional leaders.

Also in attendance were three men whom President Bush in his remarks referred to as *omonos*, the Japanese word for "heavyweights."[3] They were former Vice President Walter Mondale, former Senate majority leader Mike Mansfield, and former House Speaker Tom Foley. All three had preceded Howard Baker as ambassador to Japan. The president praised the *omonos*, and said that their presence indicated that "we send the very best people to Japan because the United States has no more important partner in the world than Japan. Our alliance is rooted in the vital strategic and economic interest that we share. It is the cornerstone of peace and prosperity in Asia."

In his remarks after being sworn in, the new ambassador returned to one of his favorite themes—bipartisanship. But now he was talking about it in the context of the working relationship between nations:

> . . . There is a special, unique relationship that exists between the United States and Japan.
>
> It is remarkable, indeed, that given our history and relationship, that Japan and the United States

would develop this strong bond, this mutuality of respect, this shared common view of the necessity for peace in the world.

My friend, Mike Mansfield, and one of my predecessors in this office, was fond of saying the bilateral relationship between the United States and Japan is the most important bilateral relationship in the world, bar none. And I always wondered, Mr. Ambassador, how "bar none" got translated into Japanese. But, Mike Mansfield, I agree with you, it is indeed the most important bilateral relationship, at least in my life and in my career, and it will continue to be. It is the cornerstone of our policy, not only in Japan but in Asia, as well, and throughout the world.[4]

The new ambassador had a deep and personal understanding of the bilateral relationship between the United States and Japan. Even before his appointment as ambassador, he had been helping build that relationship for over a decade.

In April 1989, President George Herbert Walker Bush had dispatched Baker to Japan as a de-facto special emissary.[5]

In 1988, the Reagan administration had signed a deal with the Japanese government for the development of a new Japanese fighter plane called the FSX. But the proposal had run into fierce opposition in Congress, forcing the new Bush administration to put plans on hold. The Japanese prime minister was highly offended, saying, "the maintenance of a relationship of trust" between Japan and the United States was at stake.

As a special emissary, Howard Baker used his strategic civility to reduce the tension between United States and Japan as the new administration sought to assuage congressional concerns over the proposed joint venture.

In 1991, Howard Baker had been named chair of a study group regarding the Japan-US alliance by the Council on Foreign Relations.[6]

In 1992, the future ambassador had summarized much of the work of the study group in a seventeen-page article he wrote for *Foreign Affairs*, the scholarly journal considered the nation's most authoritative foreign policy publication. In the comprehensive article, Baker and co-author Ellen Frost had painstakingly analyzed the developing tensions between the United States and Japan and had outlined proposals to establish closer economic and political links between the two countries.[7]

Throughout the decades of the 1990s, Baker's law practice had focused on US-Japanese relations, with the firm of Baker, Worthington, Crosley, Stansberry, and Wolff representing Japanese clients doing business with American firms, and American businesses wishing to invest in Japan.[8] Baker's legal work in this area had actually started in 1985 when he teamed up with his longtime aide A.B. Culvahouse at the firm of Vinson and Elkins. From 1985 to 1987, Baker and Culvahouse had represented major US firms seeking to do business in Japan.

In 2000, Howard Baker launched the "Japan-US Strategic Advisory," an organization composed of business leaders from the two countries, working to promote bilateral investment in the US and Japan in fields from nuclear power to the environment, shipping, and nanotechnology.

Baker had no doubt hoped to continue to promote these efforts in his new job as ambassador to Japan. Unfortunately, when Howard and Nancy Baker arrived at the US Embassy in Tokyo on July 3, 2001, the new ambassador had to address two immediate issues.

In April, a naval submarine, the *USS Greeneville*, had surfaced off the coast of Oahu directly underneath a Japanese fishing trawler. The ensuing collision had capsized the Japanese boat, killing five Japanese students and four crew members.

Two months later, a US Air Force sergeant had been charged with raping a Japanese woman on the island of Okinawa.[9] The Japanese government was seeking to have the sergeant handed over prior to his indictment, and the US military was resistant.

Both tragic events had been highly publicized by the Japanese media, causing strong anti-American sentiment.

The new ambassador responded with strategic civility.

First, he arranged for an invitation to a memorial service for the nine victims of the collision between the *USS Greeneville* and the fishing trawler. He and Nancy Baker attended the service, but the new ambassador did not make a speech. He met quietly with each grieving relative, shook their hand, expressed his sincere regret, and thanked them for letting him and his wife be present.

Ambassador Baker then met with Japanese Prime Minister Junichiro Koizumi and candidly discussed with him the issues underlying the alleged abuse of the Japanese woman by the American serviceman. The ambassador promised to do everything in his power to see to it that such an incident would not happen again. He then noted that under the Japan-US Status of Forces Agreement, the US military was not required to hand over military suspects before they were indicted. But here again, he promised the prime minister that he would work to resolve this matter.[10]

Over time, the ambassador was able to resolve the conflict, working on an arrangement to have the sergeant handed over to Japanese officials after his indictment.

Having resolved these initial challenges, Baker sought to build working relationships with Japanese political and business leaders, just as he had reached out to his fellow senators during his years as minority and majority leader.[11] He met at least once a week with Yasuo Fukuda, the Japanese prime minister's chief cabinet secretary. Baker's political instincts told him that Fukuda was destined to be prime minister of Japan, and it was important for the United States to build a strong relationship with him. The ambassador's political hunch was right, as Fukuda was elected Japanese prime minister in 2007.

But during their four years in Japan, Nancy and Howard Baker did more than tend to affairs of state.

They immersed themselves in the life of Japan.

They travelled throughout the nation, spending as much time as possible with ordinary people. They enjoyed visiting flea markets in Harajuku or having a drink at a Yakitori pub.

Nancy Baker became particularly fond of Japanese ice cream.[12] She worked diligently to learn Japanese, invariably expressing words of thanks such as *gochisosama deshita* (thank you for the food).

The ambassador also tried to learn the language, but he was decidedly less fluent. He later admitted that after living nearly four years in Tokyo, the only Japanese he mastered was *domo domo*.

There were actually two ambassadors living in the ambassador's residence in Akasaka, Tokyo, from 2001 to 2005. The first, of course, was Howard Baker. The second was a Wheaton Terrier puppy that Nancy and Howard Baker welcomed as a new member to their Japanese household. Nancy Baker named the pup *Taishi*, the Japanese word for ambassador.[13]

In June of 2002, the Bakers and Taishi hosted a visitor, the ambassador's old friend, President George Herbert Walker Bush.[14] The president had been a naval aviator during World War II and had been shot down by the Japanese military. The president had been rescued by a US submarine that was patrolling in the area. He climbed on a small raft provided by the submarine and was carried to safety on a nearby island.

Nearly sixty years later, the president had returned to Japan to see his friend, Ambassador Baker. The former president and the current ambassador rented a small boat that took them to the location where young George Bush had been shot down. To commemorate the occasion, the president re-enacted the event by climbing out of the boat into a small life raft.

As always, the ambassador had his Leica camera with him and took photographs of the re-enactment. As he did so, he marveled about the course of history that had transformed the United States and Japan from enemies to allies.

In early 2009, four years after his ambassadorship ended, Howard Baker was back in Huntsville. He decided to write a book to the people of Japan. The book was entitled *My Recollections: The Spirit of Bipartisanship*, and it is the closest thing to a memoir Howard Baker ever wrote. The book was published by Nikkei Publishing in Japan and was a bilingual product, containing texts in both Japanese and English in a single volume.

At the conclusion of the book, America's 38th ambassador to Japan wrote:

> Japan and the United States are very dissimilar countries. Their cultures and the systems they have created are completely different. Yet the politicians, bureaucrats, and citizens that are turned out in great numbers by both countries have a profound understanding of the significance of this special relationship and have created much new history and ties.
>
> This could be called "the spirit of bipartisanship" in foreign affairs that transcends national borders and differences between countries. It is my heartfelt hope that this spirit will long be nurtured in each of our countries.[15]

It was once again a statement of Howard Baker's civility, and this time, that civility had been played out on the world stage.

Senator Baker and Senator Bob Dole. Reprinted with the permission of the Bipartisan Policy Center.

"Public life, in its every aspect, is a collaborative enterprise."
—*Howard Baker*

CHAPTER 25

A Bipartisan Celebration

For one evening, there was a brief truce in the ongoing political civil war in Washington, DC.

On the night of March 21, 2012, a capacity crowd gathered in the Andrew Mellon Auditorium to attend "A Century of Service," a gala honoring Senator Howard Baker and Senator Bob Dole.[1]

The event was sponsored by the Bipartisan Policy Center, a Washington, DC-based think tank that was created in 2007 by four former majority leaders of the United States Senate: Republicans Baker and Dole, and Democrats Tom Daschle and George Mitchell.

Howard Baker was fond of saying that "public life, in its every aspect, is a collaborative enterprise."[2] In the creation of the Bipartisan Policy Center, Baker and his Democratic and Republican co-founders sought to promote collaboration in addressing the issues facing the nation. The center brings together former elected and appointed officials, business and labor leaders, academics, and advocates from across the political spectrum.

The Bipartisan Policy Center is not the only institute Howard Baker created to promote bipartisan policy solutions.

In early 2003, the Howard H. Baker Jr. Center for Public Policy opened on "The Hill," the campus of the University of Tennessee. Over half a century earlier, a young Howard Baker had launched his first political campaign for president of the student body.

At the Baker Center, bright students designated as Baker Scholars and educators serving as Baker Fellows engage in education and research projects designed to promote "policy and politics through a non-partisan lens."[3]

The Bipartisan Policy Center's creation only a few years later emphasized Baker's commitment to his legacy of bipartisanship and civility in public life.

The think tank's salute to founders Howard Baker and Bob Dole was truly a bipartisan event.

The first speaker was Vice President Joe Biden, a man never at a loss for words.

In his remarks, the vice president focused on what he believed was the key to Baker's effective leadership. Turning to Baker, the vice president said:

> I think you made such an exceptional leader, Howard, because of your ability to put yourself in the other guy's or other woman's shoes. I watched you, whether you and I were traveling abroad together or on the Senate floor.
>
> You always worked from the perspective of the other guy, the other woman, and how you could work out an honorable compromise.
>
> My dad used to say, "Never back another man in a corner where his only way out is over you."
>
> You never did that . . . Harry Truman could have been talking about you when he said, "When

you understand the other fellow's viewpoint and he understands yours, then you can sit down and you can work out your differences."[4]

Baker Policy Center co-founder and former Senate majority leader Tom Daschle also spoke of Baker's talent as "the great conciliator."

"Whether he was representing Tennessee in the Senate or America in Japan or steering the Reagan White House, Howard Baker was able to help everyone find common ground, without anyone feeling they were sacrificing common ground, because he is a true conciliator," Daschle said.

Former President Bill Clinton provided a film tribute, praising Baker and Dole for "their vision in establishing the Bipartisan Policy Center," and stating that the center was "a testament to their lifelong commitment to collaboration and dialogue." He added, "It's a vision we need today more than ever."

Senate leaders Harry Reid and Mitch McConnell provided tributes as did former leaders Trent Lott and Bill Frist.

Tennessee's senior senator, Lamar Alexander, spoke in honor of his longtime mentor, and in the process he proved he had been a very good student. Senator Alexander did something he had seen Baker do time and time again over the years. He told a story.

Senator Alexander told a story about how as a young man he was hired as a legislative assistant by Senator Baker. One of his first assignments was to write a speech the senator was to deliver at an event back in Tennessee. Alexander had worked diligently, crafting the words as if he were writing a State of the Union address. When Alexander proudly presented his boss with the speech transcript, Senator Baker invited his young assistant to attend the speech.

Absolutely thrilled, Alexander had accompanied the senator to the event and had sat in the audience, anxiously waiting to hear the senator read his words. But when the senator delivered his speech, he didn't use one word of the script Alexander had written.

Shortly thereafter, Baker asked his young assistant to write another speech. Alexander doubled down to make this speech better than the one that had not been delivered.

But when Alexander sat in the audience for the second speech, he again was disappointed that his boss did not use one word Alexander had written.

Crestfallen, Alexander met with his boss and said, "Senator, I think we have a real problem here. I mean, I'm working hard on these speeches, and I give them to you, and I've gone to hear them, and you don't use one word of my speeches."

Alexander recalled that Baker leaned back in his chair, laughed, and said, "Lamar, we have a perfect working relationship. You get to write what you want to write, and I get to say what I want to say."[5]

Finally, at the end of a long evening of tributes, Baker was given the floor. He had been an eloquent listener all night and he made his remarks very brief. He praised his friend Bob Dole, thanked the speakers, and then thanked everyone who worked at the Bipartisan Policy Center for making "a great contribution to the future course and direction of the country."

And then, the senator brought his remarks to a sudden conclusion. Holding up a copy of his prepared speech, he said, "To spare you the details of these remarks . . . in the best traditions of the Senate, I ask unanimous consent that my remarks be included in the record."

His father-in-law would have been proud. At eighty-six, Howard Baker was still giving himself the luxury of an unexpressed thought.

CHAPTER 26

Is 'Bakeritis' Fatal?

When Senator Trent Lott was serving as majority leader, he was contacted by a number of his constituents who were unhappy with a vote he had cast in the Senate.

They chided the majority leader for having developed an affliction they called "Bakeritis."

Their comment was not intended as a compliment. They were concerned that, like Howard Baker, Senator Trent Lott was becoming a conciliator.

Somehow word of Lott's new medical condition got back to the man for whom the affliction was named. Baker called Lott to see how he was feeling, and how his condition was progressing.

Lott laughed and said to his old Senate colleague, "I just have one question. Is 'Bakeritis' fatal?"[1]

It is a question that remains unanswered in the current political environment.

Could a candidate with the civility of Howard Baker now be elected to public office? And if so, could his or her efforts at bipartisanship work in a political culture where, in the words of former Federal Reserve Chairman Alan Greenspan, the word *compromise* has become a synonym for *treason*?

Wall Street Journal columnist and former presidential speech writer Peggy Noonan was skeptical that a candidate running on a platform of civility and bipartisanship could now be elected.

In a column written during the uncivil political summer of 2012, Noonan shared the story of a meeting she had held with a Republican candidate for Senate. She asked him to outline his plan to appeal to voters.

"The candidate leaned forward," Noonan recalled, "and said with some intensity, 'I'm going to tell people I can get along with people. I'm going to tell people I can work with the other side.'" [2]

Noonan, the brilliant speech writer who crafted the elder President Bush's phrase, "a thousand points of light," saw an inherent problem in this approach. A campaign promise of civility and bipartisanship was, she wrote, "a great example of confusing the cart with the horse. Why would anyone vote for you, especially during a crisis, only because you play well with other children?"

Recent history would confirm Noonan's doubts.

In a 2011 poll, eighty-three percent of Americans indicated that "people should not vote for candidates and politicians who are not civil."

But the real polls—election results—prove otherwise. While voters claim they don't like uncivil candidates, they vote for them.

In 2010, a candidate for Congress in a Republican primary in Howard Baker's Tennessee said in a radio interview that if elected he would "reach out across the congressional aisle to Democrats and work with them to solve the nation's problems."

His opponent immediately pounced on the statement, featuring it on a TV commercial with the tagline, "Is this really the type of person we want to send to Washington?"

On Election Day, the voters answered. By a wide margin, they rejected the candidate who had promised bipartisanship.

For over thirty years, Senator Richard Lugar of Indiana was admired in Washington for his affable and congenial style. But his bipartisanship became an issue when the senator ran for re-election in 2012. His opponent, Richard Mourdock, said that his definition of bipartisanship, in contrast to that of Richard Lugar, was "when Democrats agree with me." Mourdock defeated Senator Lugar in a landslide.

In four campaigns for the United States Senate and one campaign for the GOP presidential nomination, Baker never ran a negative ad.[3] When his opponent for the Senate in 1978 ran ads attacking him for "giving away the Panama Canal," Baker would not even respond to the charge. But would such a civil campaign possibly work in an era of attack ads and super PACS? Voters claim to be turned off by negative political ads. But politicians run them for a reason. They work.

Even if a candidate with Baker's kind of civility could be elected, his efforts at bipartisanship might still be doomed to failure.

"These days a lot of fellows come to Washington having already signed a pledge as to what they are going to do when they get here," Senator Bob Dole observed in an interview. "When you sign a pledge before you get here promising that you will never vote for a tax increase . . . Well, I'm not sure Howard or I could ever lead those people in the Senate."[4]

But Baker's friend, John Seigenthaler, believed that the civil Baker style can and should make a comeback.

"You would have to make it the centerpiece of a campaign," he said. "I think people would be receptive to hearing a man or a woman come out and say that our federal government is now dysfunctional, and we must work together to change that."[5]

Baker's friend and favorite Episcopal priest, Jack Danforth, also believed a Howard Baker-style candidate could win.

"The challenge would be to win the primary," Danforth has observed. "But if a candidate like Howard Baker survives the primary, he would be very appealing to voters in a general election."

Danforth then laughed and added, "If I were thirty years younger, I'd sure give it a try."[6]

At this point, however, the question of whether Bakeritis is fatal is a purely academic one.

No candidate is emerging on the national scene expressing the perspective that the other fellow may be right.

No candidate is coming forward promising a decent respect for the other point of view.

No candidate is promising to be an eloquent listener who will enjoy the luxury of an unexpressed thought.

But if such a candidate does someday emerge on the national political scene, she or he will have a role model.

Howard Baker is and will be the exemplar that strategic civility is strength, not weakness, and compromise is patriotism, not treason.

If and when such candidates come forward, there will remain one final unanswered question: Will we the people have the courage to vote for them?

EPILOGUE

Baker School Will Keep Senator's Legacy Alive

Senator Howard Baker passed away on June 26, 2014, at the age of 88.

The famed statesman had a profound impact on American policy. Perhaps his most outstanding legacy was in setting a model of bipartisanship in the way that our nation should be governed.

That legacy is alive today at his beloved alma mater, the University of Tennessee. It is the Howard H. Baker Jr. School of Public Policy and Public Affairs.[1]

In 2003, the senator spearheaded the institute originally called the Howard Baker Center for Public Policy. In 2023, the center expanded its mission, changing its name as it became a school within the university.

From the outset, the center encouraged bipartisanship and civility in public life.

In January 2008, Senator Baker called on his friend John Seigenthaler, who had become director of the First Amendment

Center at Vanderbilt University in Nashville. The Baker Center and the First Amendment Center co-hosted the first meeting of a task force on civility. The group was comprised of leaders from business, non-profits, academia, the press, and government, and its mission was to create a series of real-world solutions to the biggest problem facing American public life—the lack of civility in public discourse.

After months of meetings and research, the task force published *Civility in Government: Principles and Exemplars*, outlining the basic tenants of civility that should be applied in American public life. The core principle was, in Senator Baker's words, "a decent respect for different points of view."

Throughout its history, the center has built "high-quality, unique, and interdisciplinary initiatives in research, teaching, and public engagement focused on providing critical insights on domestic and international challenges. The center's work has been motivated by a vision of sound policy, thoughtful leadership, and informed citizens," according to a white paper on the facility.

In other words, the center seeks to instill in its students—the future generation of America's leaders—the values Senator Baker lived in his public life, and to promote such values in current leaders as well.

In 2022, a UT task force mapped out a new vision for the center. The next year, it became the Howard H. Baker Jr. School of Public Policy and Public Affairs.

The task force said this new school could build upon the original center's strengths in key areas: energy, mobility, environmental policy, global security, and foreign affairs.

The school would position UT "to produce the next generation of public servants and civic leaders, to conduct research on the state's most pressing challenges, and to consistently engage in productive public deliberation and problem solving," the task force concluded.

President Gerald Ford, Senator Howard Baker, and President Jimmy Carter. Reprinted with the permission of Senator Baker and the Baker Center.

The Baker School will expand the former center's work through programs such as:

• **Baker Scholars.** This program consists of UT's most academically gifted and politically curious students.

Each Baker Scholar researches a significant public policy issue, and each student will be paired in research with faculty or professional mentors.

• **Japan Ambassadors.** The school will also provide plenty of opportunities to learn by doing.

The ambassadors program is a twelve-day international experience for students to follow in Baker's footsteps. Students learn about Japanese culture, international affairs, foreign policy, and diplomatic relations between the US and Japan.

• **Washington Fellows.** In our nation's capital, this program is a two-week intensive course in which students meet with some of the nation's top public servants, journalists, and researchers. They develop policy briefs on issues.

• **Institute on American Civics.** The Baker School will also promote education as the home of the new Institute on American Civics, a Tennessee program meant to advance civics education and engagement and to promote civil discourse—with Senator Baker's public life as a model.

• **New research centers.** The Baker School will also have new research centers: Energy, Transportation, and Environmental Policy, and National Security and Foreign Affairs. Both centers focus on areas that speak directly to Baker's legacy.

Among the energy and environmental issues being researched are energy consumption and conservation, renewable energy, air and water pollution, and climate change. The national security research program honors Senator Baker's service as a Naval officer, White House chief of staff, and ambassador to Japan. Among the issues researched are international and civil conflict resolution, maritime and territorial disputes, terrorism and other political violence, nuclear security, and proliferation.

* * *

Senator Howard Baker was dedicated to finding ways for people to work together, respecting different points of view, translating disagreements into resolution, and finding solutions to the issues that confront us.

That is the legacy he left us.

The Baker School will strive to preserve and strengthen his spirit of diplomacy and bipartisan leadership.

ACKNOWLEDGMENTS

I'm neither a scholar nor a journalist. I am a lawyer who likes to write and tell stories about inspirational people. For nearly 50 years, I have been inspired by Senator Howard Baker. I first met him in 1973 when I was an undergraduate at the University of Tennessee and had just been elected president of the student body. I was introduced to Senator Baker at the UT Student Center by Trustee Ann Baker Furrow. Senator Baker shook my hand and said, "Bill, you are holding the only office I ever held in life other than United States senator."

It was heady stuff for a twenty-one-year-old boy from Memphis. Although my own political career began and ended with college student government, I continued to follow and be inspired by Senator Baker over the years.

While I am not a scholar, my good friend Carl Pierce is. As director emeritus of the Howard Baker Center for Public Policy at the University of Tennessee, Professor Pierce supported me in every step of the way in my research and writing of this book.

Former Baker Center Director Matt Murray and Associate Director Nissa Dahlin-Brown were also incredibly supportive. They opened the doors of the Baker Center archives to me as if I really were a scholar, rather than just a lawyer who likes to write.

Baker Center Director Marianne Wanamaker was particularly helpful to me as I wrote the epilogue on the center's evolution to become the Howard Baker School of Public Policy in 2023.

And on the same campus affectionately known to Senator Baker and me as "The Hill," I've had the unfailing support of Dr. Keith Carver and Vice Chancellor Margie Nichols.

I am also indebted to another true scholar, J. Lee Annis Jr., the author of the definitive biography of Senator Howard Baker, *Howard Baker: Conciliator In An Age of Crisis*. As reflected in the notes section, Professor Annis's book was a major reference source for this book, and it is a must-read for anyone who wants to study the remarkable life of Senator Howard Baker.

And while I am not a journalist, I am grateful for the time and support that was given to me by two incredible Tennessee journalists, the late John Seigenthaler and Tom Griscom.

The second person I interviewed for this book, after Senator Baker, was the late Lewis Donelson. This remarkable man was the architect of the two-party system in Tennessee, and without his support, this book would not have been possible.

I am also grateful to many of Senator Baker's contemporaries in public life including Senator John Danforth, Senator Lamar Alexander, Senator Richard Lugar, Governor Winfield Dunn, Congressman Bill Jenkins, A.B. Culvahouse, the late Judge Harry Wellford, the late John Waters, and the late Senator Fred Thompson. All spent many hours telling me stories about their dear friend, Howard Baker.

Senator Baker's long-time personal assistant and close friend, Fred Marcum, spent many hours reviewing my manuscript and giving me wonderful suggestions.

My dear late friend Pam Reeves and Charles Swanson literally fed and housed me during my work on this book. I've also had the encouragement and support of many other friends including Dawn LaFon, the late and wonderful Roy Herron, Lucian Pera, Jane Van Daren, Nick McCall, Charles Huddleston, Loretta Harber, Sarah Sheppeard, Ben Alford, Justice Sharon Lee, Allan

Ramsaur, Suzanne Robertson, Inman Majors, Keel Hunt, Hal Hardin, Buck Lewis, Buck Wellford, Sam Elliott, Chris Vescovo and Jason Long.

Thanks to my personal assistants Renata Sadetsky and Sandy White, and to my research assistants, Julie Bixby, Reedy Swanson, Grayson Schleppegrell, and Michael Nelson.

Thanks to my editor and publisher, the remarkable Jacque Hillman.

Finally, I must thank two extraordinary women. The first made me start this book, and the second made me finish it. The book was the idea of my late mother-in-law, Claude Galbreath Swafford, to whom this book is posthumously dedicated. She was a classmate of Senator Howard Baker in the University of Tennessee Law School Class of 1949. For reasons I still don't understand, she suggested years ago that I write this book, and kept bringing it up at Christmas dinner and family reunions each year until I finally gave in and started it.

And the second is the love of my life, Claudia Swafford Haltom, who while acknowledging that her husband is neither a scholar nor a journalist, does tell me that I tell great stories.

I hope after reading this book, you agree.

SOURCES

Interviews Conducted by the Author

Senator Howard Baker
Senator Lamar Alexander
A.B. Culvahouse
Senator John Danforth
Senator Robert Dole
Lewis Donelson
Governor Winfield Dunn
Tom Griscom
Jim Haslam
Congressman Bill Jenkins
John Seigenthaler
Don Stansberry
Lonnie Strunk
Bill Swain
Senator Fred Thompson
John Tuck
John Waters
Judge Harry Wellford
Bob Worthington

Baker Center Oral History Project Interviews

Cissy Baker
Senator Bill Brock
Senator Dale Bumpers
Vice President Richard Cheney
Alexander Haig
Dr. Joe Johnson
Nancy Kassebaum Baker
Congressman Dan Kuykendall
Senator Russell Long
Edwin Meese

Tennessee Bar Foundation Oral History Project

Interview with Senator Baker by Robert Worthington, September 6, 2006.

University of Tennessee Interview

"A Conversation with Howard Baker Jr. and John Seigenthaler," September 30, 2005.

Tennessee Bar Association Interview

Freedom's Foundation, television interview with Senator Howard Baker, August 2005.

BOOKS

Annis Jr., J. Lee, *Howard Baker: Conciliator in an Age of Crisis*. Madison Books, 1995.
Baker, Howard, *No Margin for Error: America in the Eighties*. Times Books, 1980.
Baker, Howard, *My Recollections: The Spirit of Bipartisanship*. Nikkei Publishing, 2009.
Baker, Howard, *Howard Baker's Washington*. Norton, 1982.
Baker, Howard and John Netherton, *Big South Fork Country*. Rutledge Hill Press, 1993.
Danforth, John, *Faith and Politics*. Viking, 2006.
Dirksen, Luella, *The Honorable Mr. Marigold: My Life with Everett Dirksen*. Doubleday, 1972.
Donelson, Lewis, *Lewie*. Rhodes College, 2012.
Dunn, Winfield, *From a Standing Start: My Tennessee Political Odyssey*. Magellan Press, 2007.
Hulsey, Byron, *Everett Dirksen and His Presidents: How a Senate Giant Shaped American Politics*. University of Kansas, 2000.
Shapiro, Ira, *The Last Great Senate: Courage and Statesmanship in Times of Crisis*. Public Affairs, 2012.
Thompson, Fred, *At That Point in Time: The Inside Story of the Senate Watergate Committee*. Quadrangle New York Times Books, 1975.
Waters Jr., John B., *Down Bound: The Memoirs of John Waters*. Nexus, 2000.

ARTICLES

Annis Jr., J. Lee, "Howard H. Baker Jr.: A Life in Public Service," *Baker Center Journal of Applied Public Policy* (Fall 2012).
Baker, Russell, "One Man Is an Island," *New York Times*, March 3, 1987.
Baker, Howard and Ellen Frost, "Rescuing the US Japan Alliance," *Foreign Affairs* (Spring 1992).
Broder, David, "Baker Leading the Senate," *Washington Post*, March 18, 1981.
Brown Jr., Theodore, "Howard H. Baker Jr. and the Public Values of Cooperation and Civility," *Baker Center Journal of Applied Public Policy* (Fall 2012).
Cohen, David B. and Charles Walcott, "Cinncinatus of Tennessee: Howard Baker as White House Chief of Staff," *Baker Center Journal of Applied Public Policy* (Fall 2012).
Deward, Helen, "The Charmer from Tennessee," *Washington Post*, February 16, 1982.

Dowd, Maureen, "The Reagan White House: A Love-In for Baker at the Capitol," *New York Times*, March 5, 1987.
Eisenhower, David, "Howard Baker: Fighting the President's Final Battles," *New York Times Magazine*, September 6, 1987.
Farney, Dennis, "Baker is Ready for Civilian Life," *Wall Street Journal*, August 8, 1984.
Hamilton, James, "The Senate Watergate Committee: Its Place in History and the Discovery of the White House Tapes," *Baker Center Journal of Applied Public Policy* (Fall 2012).
Noonan, Peggy, "A Nation That Believes in Nothing," *Wall Street Journal*, August 11, 2012.
Reston, James, "Washington Talk: Q & A With Howard Baker Jr.," *New York Times*, May 12, 1987.
Reston, James, "Howard Baker As Veep," *New York Times*, June 19, 1988.
Roberts, Steven V., "Aides Say Baker Felt Task Unfinished," *New York Times*, June 16, 1988.
Roberts, Steven V., "We Must Not Be Enemies: Howard Baker Jr. and the Role of Civility in Politics," *Baker Center Journal of Applied Public Policy* (Fall 2012).
Schiller, Wendy, "Howard Baker's Leadership in the United States Senate: Lessons in Persuasion, Civility and Success," *Baker Center Journal of Applied Public Policy* (Fall 2012).
Tolchin, Martin, "Howard Baker Jr. Finds There is Life After the Senate," *New York Times*, April 29, 1985.
Lamar, Jacob, "The Right Man at the Right Time," *Time*, March 9, 1987.
Lee, Gary, "Japan Article, A Question of Partiality," *Washington Post*, May 13, 1992.
Lindsay, Powell, "Ain't No Love in Baker Courtin," *Knoxville News Sentinel*, March 24, 1967.
McPherson, Myra, "What the Well-Dressed Senator Wears on the Tennis Court," *New York Times*, September 29, 1967.
Weinraub, Bernard, "The White House Crisis: Regan's Exit Was Inevitable, Baker's Entrance a Surprise," *New York Times*, March 1, 1987.
Wicker, Tom, "Desperately Seeking Iowa," *New York Times*, February 4, 1988.
Editorial, "Howard Baker's Selfless Service," *New York Times*, June 16, 1988.
"Talking Politics: Howard Baker Jr.," *New York Times*, January 18, 1980.
"The Basic Speech: Howard Baker Jr.," *New York Times*, March 1, 1980.

SPEECHES BY SENATOR HOWARD BAKER

"Cleaning America's Air—Progress and Challenges," University of Tennessee, March 9, 2005, www.muskiefoundation.org./baker030905.html.

"The View from Both Ends of Pennsylvania Avenue," Center for the Study of the Presidency, 1990.

"The United States and Its Global Role," Speech at the World Trade Center of New Orleans, June 9, 2005, Howard Baker Center Archives.

"Farewell Address to the United States Senate," *Congressional Record*, October 12, 1984.

"The Role of the Senate," *Congressional Record*, April 6, 1989.

"On Herding Cats," United States Senate Lecture Series, July 14, 1998.

"Remarks on Senate Ratification of the Panama Canal Treaties," *Congressional Record*, February 9, 1978.

"US Senate Watergate Committee Opening Statement," *Congressional Record*, May 17, 1973.

"The Highest Secular Calling," Lecture, University of Louisville Law School, March 28, 2005.

OTHER SOURCES

"A Century of Service: A Tribute to Senators Howard Baker and Bob Dole," Bipartisan Policy Center, March 22, 2012.

The Almanac of American Politics, Editions 1972, 1974, 1976, 1978, 1980.

Civility in Government: Principles and Exemplars. Howard H. Baker Jr. Center for Public Policy, 2007. V.

Howard H. Baker Jr. School of Public Policy and Public Affairs, baker.utk.edu.

Senno, Hadil, "The Great Conciliator and US Foreign Policy: Learning from Senator Howard Baker's Example During the Panama Canal Treaties Ratification," Howard Baker Scholars Research Paper, 2012.

The World Almanac and Book of Facts, Editions 1982 and 1988.

NOTES

PROLOGUE

1. "Our President Wants Us Here: The Mob That Stormed The Capitol," *New York Times*, January 10, 2021.
2. "Trump Capitol Riot: Police Officer Suicides Rise to Four Deaths," CNBC, August 2, 2021.
3. "How A Pro-Trump Mob Stormed the Capitol," *New York Times*, January 7, 2021.
4. "Trump Refuses to Accept Election Results, Says It Is Far From Over," CNBC, November 7, 2020.
5. "Trump and GOP Have Lost More Than 50 Post-Election Lawsuits," *Forbes*, December 9, 2020.
6. "What Trump Told Supporters Before Many Stormed Capitol Hill," *ABC News*, January 7, 2021.
7. "Incitement to Riot? What Trump Told Supporters Before Mob Stormed The Capitol," *New York Times*, January 12, 2021.
8. "January 6th Capitol Attack," *Encyclopedia Brittanica*.
9. Ibid.
10. "Shame Nation: The Rise of Incivility in America," *Huffington Post*, June 13, 2017.
11. "Founder Of Civility Project Calls It Quits," *New York Times*, January 12, 2011.
12. Tom Brokaw, *The Greatest Generation* (Dell, 1998).

CHAPTER 1: A Civil Moment

1. Ira Shapiro, *The Last Great Senate: Courage and Statesmanship in Times of Crisis* (Public Affairs, 2012).
2. *The US Senate Republican Leader's Suite*, Senate Publication 110-6.
3. Ibid.
4. "Tennessee Charmer Howard Baker leads the Senate his way," *Washington Post*, February 16, 1982.

5. J. Lee Annis Jr., *Howard Baker: Conciliator in an Age of Crisis* (Howard H. Baker Jr. Center for Public Policy, 2007), 30.
6. David Broder, "Apportionment Honors Due Senators Kennedy and Baker," *Washington Post*, November 14, 1967.
7. Steven V. Roberts, "We Must Not Be Enemies: Howard H. Baker Jr. and The Role of Civility in Politics," *Baker Center Journal of Applied Public Policy*, Vol. 4, No. II (Fall 2012).
8. *The Almanac of American Politics 1978* (Sunrise, 1978).
9. *Civility in Government: Principles and Exemplars* (Howard H. Baker Jr. Center for Public Policy, 2007), V.
10. Jeffrey Rosen, "Justice Howard Baker," *Baker Center Journal of Applied Public Policy*, 49.
11. Interview with A.B. Culvahouse, July 7, 2012.
12. Shapiro, *The Last Great Senate*.
13. Ibid.
14. Ibid.
15. Ibid.
16. Ibid.
17. Interview with Senator Howard Baker, February 27, 2012.
18. Ibid.
19. *Civility in Government* (Howard H. Baker Jr. Center for Public Policy, 2007), iii.

CHAPTER 2: A Father's Advice

1. Interview with Senator Howard Baker by Robert Worthington, Tennessee Bar Foundation Oral History Project, September 6, 2006.
2. Ibid.
3. Annis Jr., *Howard Baker: Conciliator*.
4. Ibid.
5. Ibid.
6. "Lilly Mauser, 101 and ex-sheriff, grandmother of Senator Baker," *New York Times*, April 21, 1981.
7. "Will Scott County Secede Again?" *Tennessee Bar Journal*, January 2013.
8. Annis Jr., *Howard Baker: Conciliator*.
9. Baker interview, February 27, 2012.
10. Ibid.

CHAPTER 3: The Education of a Civil Man

1. Annis Jr., *Howard Baker: Conciliator*, 5-6.
2. Baker interview, Worthington.
3. Annis Jr., *Howard Baker: Conciliator*, 5-6.
4. Baker interview, Worthington.
5. Ibid.
6. Annis Jr., *Howard Baker: Conciliator*, 6.
7. Baker interview, Worthington.
8. Howard Baker, "The United States and Its Global Role," Speech at the World Trade Center, New Orleans, Louisiana, June 9, 2005, Howard Baker Center Archives.
9. Ibid.
10. Ibid.
11. Ambassador Howard Baker, Speech on the *USS Kitty Hawk*, April 5, 2002, Howard Baker Center Archives.
12. Baker interview, Worthington.
13. Baker interview, Worthington.
14. Annis Jr., *Howard Baker: Conciliator*, 6.
15. Interview with John B. Waters, May 7, 2012.
16. *The Orange and White*, April 27, 1948.
17. Annis Jr., *Howard Baker: Conciliator*, 7.

CHAPTER 4: Civil Litigation

1. "What Hath Scopes Wrought?" *Tennessee Bar Journal*, Vol. 41, No. 8, August 2005.
2. Interview with Don Stansberry, August 4, 2012.
3. Baker interview, Worthington.
4. Annis Jr., *Howard Baker: Conciliator*, 7.
5. Ibid, 11.
6. Baker interview, February 27, 2012.
7. Baker interview, Worthington.
8. Annis Jr., *Howard Baker: Conciliator*, 7.
9. Baker interview, Worthington.
10. Interview with Bill Swain, August 4, 2012.
11. Ibid.
12. Stansberry interview.

13. Ibid.
14. Baker interview, Worthington.
15. *Freedom's Foundation*, television program produced by Tennessee Bar Association, August 2005.
16. Annis Jr., *Howard Baker: Conciliator*, 12-13.

CHAPTER 5: A Bipartisan Coalition Begins

1. E. William Henry, *Fatal Alliance: The Prosecution, Indictment and Gangland Murder of Jimmy Hoffa* (Andover Press, 2012), 56.
2. Ibid, 57-58.
3. Ibid, xvi-xx.
4. Interview with John Seigenthaler, May 11, 2012.
5. *Tennessee Encyclopedia of History and Culture* (Rutledge Hill Press, 1998), 220-227.
6. Lewis R. Donelson, III, *Lewie* (Rhodes College Press, 2012)
7. Ibid.
8. Ibid.
9. Ibid.
10. Interview with Judge Harry Wellford, May 3, 2012.
11. Interview with Lewis Donelson, April 30, 2012.
12. Ibid.
13. Ibid.
14. Interview with John Waters.
15. Ibid.
16. Donelson interview.
17. Howard Baker, *No Margin for Error*, (Times Press, 1980), 7.
18. Wellford interview.
19. Waters interview.
20. Donelson interview.
21. Seigenthaler interview.
22. Baker, *No Margin for Error*.
23. Ibid.
24. Annis Jr., *Howard Baker: Conciliator*, 21-22.

CHAPTER 6: The Beginning of the Two-Party System

1. Lee S. Greene, *Lead Me On: Frank Goad Clement and Tennessee Politics*, (1982).

2. *Tennessee Encyclopedia of History and Culture*, 171-180.
3. Ibid.
4. *Almanac of American Politics 1974* (Gambit, 1974), 936.
5. Waters interview.
6. Baker interview, February 27, 2012.
7. Annis Jr., *Howard Baker: Conciliator*, 23.
8. Ibid, 25.
9. Wellford interview.
10. Ibid.
11. Annis Jr., *Howard Baker: Conciliator*, 27-28.
12. Ibid, 29.
13. Seigenthaler interview.
14. Donelson interview.

CHAPTER 7: The Luxury of an Unexpressed Thought

1. "The Highest Secular Calling: Personal Perspectives On Public Service," Remarks by Senator Howard Baker, Brandeis Law School, University of Louisville, March 28, 2005.
2. Ibid.
3. Ibid.
4. Ibid.
5. Ibid.
6. Byron C. Hulsey, *Everett Dirksen and His Presidents: How a Senate Giant Shaped American Politics* (University of Kansas Press, 2000).
7. Louella Dirksen, *The Honorable Mr. Marigold, My Life With Everett Dirksen* (Doubleday, 1972).
8. Hulsey, *Everett Dirksen and His Presidents*, 273.
9. Ibid.
10. Ibid, 148-149.
11. Lamar Alexander, Remarks, "A Century of Service: A Tribute to Senators Howard Baker and Bob Dole," Bipartisan Policy Center, March 22, 2012.

CHAPTER 8: An Eloquent Listener

1. Waters interview.
2. Ibid.
3. Ibid.
4. Ibid.

5. Interview with Senator Nancy Kassebaum Baker, Howard Baker Oral History Project, September 24, 1993.
6. Fred Thompson, *At That Point in Time: The Inside Story of the Senate Watergate Committee* (Quadrangle New York Times Books, 1975), 49.
7. Interview with Ron McMahon, Howard Baker Oral History Project, October 25, 1994.
8. Baker interview, February 27, 2012.

CHAPTER 9: One-Man, One-Vote, Two Senators

1. *Baker v. Carr*, 369 US 186 (March 26, 1962).
2. Gene Graham, *One Man, One Vote* (Little Brown, 1972), 3.
3. Vijaya S. Perumalla, Theodore Brown, Carl Pierce, "The Fight for One-Man, One-Vote and the Role of Senator Howard Baker Jr.," Howard H. Baker Jr. Center for Public Policy.
4. Ibid.
5. Ibid.
6. *Gray v. Sanders*, 372 US 368 (March 18, 1963).
7. *Wesberry v. Sanders*, 376 US 1 (February 17, 1964).
8. *Reynolds v. Sims*, 377 US 533 (1964).
9. Perumalla, et al., "One-Man, One-Vote."
10. Arlen Large, "Dirksen's Crusade," *Wall Street Journal*, June 2, 1967.
11. Perumalla, et al., "One-Man, One-Vote."
12. Annis Jr., *Howard Baker: Conciliator*, 33.
13. Perumalla, et al., "One-Man, One-Vote."
14. Ibid.
15. Ibid.
16. Ibid.

CHAPTER 10: Game, Set . . . Bipartisan Match

1. *Washingtonian*, April 1967.
2. Baker remarks, Congressional Record, April 17, 1967.
3. Ibid.
4. "What The Well-Dressed Senator Wears on the Tennis Court," *New York Times*, September 29, 1967.
5. "Democrats Take Senatorial Tennis Match," *Washington Post*, September 29, 1967.
6. Ibid.

CHAPTER 11: A Bipartisan Environment

1. Baker interview.
2. Howard Baker and John Netherton, *Big South Fork Country* (Rutledge Hill Press, 1993).
3. Ibid, 9.
4. Annis Jr., *Howard Baker: Conciliator*, 1.
5. Howard Baker, "Cleaning America's Air—Progress and Challenges," University of Tennessee, March 9, 2005, www.muskiefoundation.org. baker.030905.html
6. Ibid.
7. Baker and Netherton, *Big South Fork Country*, 11-12.
8. Ibid, 9.
9. Baker, "Cleaning America's Air," 3-4.
10. Ibid, 3.
11. Ibid, 2.
12. Ibid, 2.
13. Baker and Netherton, *Big South Fork Country*, 12.
14. Baker, "Cleaning America's Air," 7-8.
15. Ibid, 1.
16. Ibid, 8.

CHAPTER 12: Asking the Right Questions

1. "Highest Secular Calling," Baker remarks, March 28, 2005.
2. Annis Jr., *Howard Baker: Conciliator*, 37.
3. "Highest Secular Calling," Baker remarks, March 28, 2005.
4. Ibid.
5. Ibid.
6. Ibid.
7. Ibid.
8. Fred Thompson, *At This Point in Time*, 4.
9. Ibid.
10. "The Presidential Campaign Activities in 1972, Watergate and Related Activities," Hearing before the Senate Select Committee on Presidential Campaign Activities, 93rd Congress, Opening Statement of Senator Howard H. Baker Jr.
11. "A Century of Service," Bipartisan Policy Center.
12. Annis Jr., *Howard Baker: Conciliator*, 68.

13. Ibid.
14. "A Century of Service," Bipartisan Policy Center.
15. Fred Thompson, *At That Point in Time*, 83.
16. Ibid.
17. Ibid.
18. Ibid, 84.
19. Ibid, 89-90.
20. Ibid, 260.
21. Interview with Fred Thompson.

CHAPTER 13: An Eloquent Observer

1. "Mr. Baker's Photographic Mind," *New York Times*, January 8, 1982.
2. "Howard Baker: Trying to Tame an Unruly Senate," *New York Times Magazine*, March 28, 1982.
3. "Primary Faces and Places," Colorfax Laboratories Exhibit, 1982, Baker Center Archives.
4. Ibid.
5. "Baker is Ready for Civilian Life," *Wall Street Journal*, August 8, 1984.
6. Interview with Cissy Baker, Howard Baker Oral History Project.
7. "Baker is Ready for Civilian Life," *Wall Street Journal*, August 8, 1984.
8. John Danforth, *Faith and Politics* (Viking, 2006), 182-183.
9. Ibid.
10. Ibid, 184-185.
11. Interview with Congressman Bill Jenkins, May 3, 2012.
12. Howard Baker, *Howard Baker's Washington* (W. W. Norton and Company, 1982).
13. Ibid.
14. Ibid.

CHAPTER 14: Saving the Panama Canal

1. American Conservative Union Ad, *Tennessean*, September 4, 1977.
2. Senator Howard Baker Jr., "Remarks on Senate Ratification of the Panama Canal Treaties," 124 Cong. Rec. 3,022-25 (February 9, 1978).
3. Ibid.
4. Ibid.

5. Shapiro, *The Last Great Senate*, 135.
6. Ibid, 135-137.
7. Hadil Senno, "The Great Conciliator and US Foreign Policy: Learning from Senator Howard Baker's Example during the Panama Canal Treaties Ratification," Howard Baker Scholars research paper, 2012.
8. Ibid.
9. Baker, "Remarks on Senate Ratification of the Panama Canal Treaties."
10. Ibid.
11. Senno, "The Great Conciliator."
12. Interview with Bill Swain, August 3, 2012.
13. Senno, "The Great Conciliator."
14. Ibid.
15. Baker, "Remarks on Senate Ratification of the Panama Canal Treaties."
16. Senno, "The Great Conciliator."
17. Ibid.
18. Ibid.
19. Ibid.
20. Baker interview, February 27, 2012.

CHAPTER 15: The Unmaking of the President, 1980
1. Interview with Tom Griscom, May 7, 2012.
2. Ibid.
3. Ibid.
4. Ibid.
5. Interview with Senator John Danforth, June 11, 2012.
6. Ibid.
7. Baker, *No Margin for Error*, 3.
8. Hugh Sidey, "Senator Baker Folds his Tent with Characteristic Courage," *Washington Star*, March 9, 1980.
9. Ibid.
10. Annis Jr., *Howard Baker: Conciliator*.

CHAPTER 16: A New Office Does Not Require a New Office
1. Baker interview.
2. Annis Jr., *Howard Baker: Conciliator*, 178.
3. Ibid.

4. Lamar Alexander, Remarks, "A Century of Service."
5. David S. Broder, "Baker Leading the Senate," *Washington Post*, March 18, 1981.
6. Howard Baker, *Howard Baker's Washington*, 21.
7. Ibid, 21-25.
8. Broder, "Baker Leading the Senate."
9. Griscom interview.
10. Ibid.
11. Ibid.
12. Ibid.
13. Broder, "Baker Leading the Senate."
14. Ibid.
15. Helen Dewar, "The Charmer from Tennessee: Howard Baker Leads the Senate His Way," *Washington Post*, February 16, 1982.
16. Ibid.
17. Ibid.
18. Broder, "Baker Leading the Senate."
19. "Reagan's First Year," *The World Almanac and Book of Facts 1982*, 38.
20. Ibid.
21. John Danforth, *Faith and Politics* (Viking, 2006), 222.
22. Michael Barone and Grant Ujifusa, *The Almanac of American Politics 1982* (Barone and Company, 1982).
23. Senator Trent Lott, United States Senate Leader's Lecture Series, July 14, 1998.

CHAPTER 17: A Rose for Mrs. Packwood

1. *World Almanac and Book of Facts 1982*, 945.
2. Annis Jr., *Howard Baker: Conciliator*, 187.
3. *World Almanac and Book of Facts 1982*, 947.
4. Ibid, 945.
5. Annis Jr., *Howard Baker: Conciliator*, 187.
6. Ibid.
7. Ibid, 189.
8. Howard Baker and Nancy Kassebaum Baker, interviews.
9. Baker interview.

CHAPTER 18: The Baker's Dozen

1. Howard Baker, 130 Cong. Rec. 32,509-11 (Daily ed., October 12, 1984).
2. "Baker is Ready for Civilian Life," *Wall Street Journal*, August 8, 1984.
3. 130 Cong. Rec. 32,509.
4. Ibid.
5. Ibid.
6. Howard H. Baker Jr., "On Herding Cats," United States Senate Leaders lecture series, 1998-2002, July 14, 1998.
7. Ibid.
8. Ibid.
9. Ibid.

CHAPTER 19: Saving the President

1. Lamar Alexander, Remarks, "A Century of Service."
2. David V. Cohen and Charles E. Walcott, "Cincinnatus of Tennessee: Howard Baker as White House Chief of Staff," *Baker Center Journal of Applied Public Policy*, vol. IV, no. 2, (Fall 2012) 73.
3. John Tower, Edmund Muskie, and Brent Scowcroft, Tower Commission Report (1987).
4. Jack Anderson and Dale Van Atta, "Iran-Contra Affair," *The World Almanac and Book of Facts 1988*, 36-39.
5. Ibid.
6. Tower Commission Report.
7. Gerald Boyd, "The White House Crisis: Regan Replaced by President," *New York Times*, February 28, 1987.
8. Cohen and Walcott, "Cincinnatus of Tennessee."
9. Ibid, 71.
10. Bernard Weinraub, "The White House Crisis; Regan's Exit was Inevitable; Baker's Entrance a Surprise," *New York Times*, March 1, 1987.
11. Ibid.
12. Ibid.
13. Ibid.
14. Bernard Weinraub, "The White House Crisis."
15. Culvahouse interview.
16. Cohen and Walcott, "Cincinnatus of Tennessee."
17. Ibid.
18. Ibid.

19. Ibid.
20. Ibid.
21. Ibid, p. 79.
22. Maureen Dowd, "The Reagan White House; A Love-In for Baker at Capitol," *New York Times*, March 5, 1987.
23. Ibid.
24. Ibid.
25. Ibid.
26. Seigenthaler interview.
27. Culvahouse interview.
28. Ibid.
29. Ibid.
30. Ibid.
31. Anderson and Van Atta, "The Iran-Contra Affair," 38.
32. Ibid.
33. Ibid.
34. Report of the Congressional Committees Investigating the Iran-Contra Affair, S. Rep. No. 216, H.R. Rep. No. 433, 100th Cong. (November 18, 1987).
35. Ibid.
36. Cohen and Walcott, "Cinncinatus of Tennessee," 77.
37. Roberts, "We Must Not be Enemies," 10.
38. Ibid.
39. Cohen and Walcott, "Cinncinatus of Tennessee," 81-83.
40. Seigenthaler interview.

CHAPTER 20: A Gentle Tennessee Wit

1. Letter Accepting the Resignation of Howard H. Baker Jr. as Chief of Staff to the President, June 28, 1988, www.reagan.utexas.edu/archives.
2. Baker interview.
3. Culvahouse interview.
4. Interview with Lonnie Strunk, August 6, 2012.
5. Howard Baker, *Howard Baker's Washington*, 6.

CHAPTER 21: The View from Both Ends of Pennsylvania Avenue

1. Howard Baker Jr., Keynote Address, 21st Annual Student's Symposium of the Center for the Study of the Presidency, March 26, 1990, as published in *Presidential Studies Quarterly*, Vol. 20, No. 3 (Summer 1990): 489-92.

CHAPTER 22: The Cherry Blossom Romance

1. Annis Jr., *Howard Baker: Conciliator*, 33.
2. Howard Baker, *My Recollections: The Spirit of Bipartisanship*, (Nikkei Publishing, 2009), 8.
3. Ibid.
4. Annis Jr., *Howard Baker: Conciliator*, 96-97.
5. Ibid, 94-95.
6. Ibid, 96.
7. Ibid.
8. Ibid.
9. Ibid, 97.
10. Culvahouse interview.

CHAPTER 23: To Form a More Perfect Union

1. Baker, *My Recollections*, 52.
2. Nancy Kassebaum Baker interview, Oral History Project.
3. Baker, *My Recollections*, 63.
4. Ibid, 52.
5. Ibid, 52.
6. *New York Times*, December 8, 1996.
7. Danforth interview.
8. Annis Jr., *Howard Baker: Conciliator*, 235.

CHAPTER 24: Ambassador Baker: Civility on the World Stage

1. Office of the Press Secretary, the White House, June 26, 2001.
2. Baker, *My Recollections*, 54-55.
3. Ibid, 56.
4. Office of the Press Secretary, the White House, June 25, 2001.
5. Baker, *My Recollections*, 66.
6. Ibid.
7. Howard H. Baker Jr. and Ellen L. Frost, "Rescuing the US-Japan Alliance," *Foreign Affairs*, (1992).
8. "Japan Article: A Question of Partiality," *Washington Post*, May 13, 1992.
9. Baker, *My Recollections*, 62.
10. Ibid.
11. Ibid, 64.

12. Ibid, 61.
13. Ibid.
14. Ibid, 62-63.
15. Ibid.

CHAPTER 25: A Bipartisan Celebration

1. "A Century of Service: Honoring the Service of Senator Howard Baker and Senator Robert Dole," Federal News Service, March 21, 2012.
2. Baker, *No Margin for Error*.
3. *Civility in Government: Principles and Exemplars*, Bipartisan Policy Center, 2008.
4. "A Century of Service."
5. "A Century of Service."

CHAPTER 26: Is 'Bakeritis' Fatal?

1. Senator Trent Lott, introduction to Senator Howard Baker address, *United States Senate Leader's Series* (July 14, 1998).
2. "A Nation that Believes in Nothing," *Wall Street Journal*, August 11, 2012.
3. Donelson interview.
4. Interview with Senator Robert Dole, July 7, 2012.
5. Seigenthaler interview.
6. Danforth interview.

EPILOGUE: Baker School Will Keep Senator's Legacy Alive

1. All information from this chapter comes from the Howard H. Baker Jr. School of Public Policy and Public Affairs, bakercenter.utk.edu.

BILL HALTOM

Bill Haltom is a father, husband, lawyer, and award-winning writer. He is the author of nine books and has been a newspaper and magazine humor columnist for over twenty-five years. He has served as chair of the editorial boards for four magazines, including the ABA Journal, the flagship publication of the American Bar Association.

A popular speaker, Bill has delivered commencement addresses and has been the featured speaker at conventions, banquets, and leadership seminars.

Bill lives and writes in Memphis and Monteagle, Tennessee, with his wife, Claudia.

For more information, go to www.billhaltom.com.

"So long as the Clean Air Act, its principles and its goals survive, I will have a lasting legacy.

I have always been struck by the fact that Thomas Jefferson insisted that his tombstone reflect only that he had founded the University of Virginia—not that he was ambassador to France, or secretary of state, or vice president, or even president of the United States. Not that he had drafted the Declaration of Independence, but that he had founded an institution of higher learning.

I cannot compare my own career to Jefferson's, nor would I be so bold to say that I alone wrote the Clean Air Act. But I am willing to say and let my legacy rest on the fact that I was one of two or three American citizens who happened to be United States senators who came together at a particular moment in history and developed the concept which in many respects can be said to have changed the world in which we live. . . .

That's my legacy. I would be proud to have 'He wrote the Clean Air Act' on my tombstone."

—*Howard H. Baker Jr., excerpts from a speech titled "Cleaning America's Air—Progress and Challenges," March 9, 2005, at the University of Tennessee Knoxville. www.muskiefoundation.org. baker.030905.html*

www.ingramcontent.com/pod-product-compliance
Lightning Source LLC
Chambersburg PA
CBHW051620010526
44119CB00009B/215